SSAT Lower Level Math workbook

Math Exercises, Activities, and Two Full-Length SSAT Lower Level Math Practice Tests

By

Michael Smith & Reza Nazari

SSAT Lower Level Math Workbook

Published in the United State of America By

The Math Notion

Email: info@Mathnotion.com

Web: www.MathNotion.com

About the Author

Michael Smith has been a math instructor for over a decade now. He holds a master's degree in Management. Since 2006, Michael has devoted his time to both teaching and developing exceptional math learning materials. As a Math instructor and test prep expert, Michael has worked with thousands of students. He has used the feedback of his students to develop a unique study program that can be used by students to drastically improve their math score fast and effectively.

– **SAT Math Workbook**

– **PSAT Math Workbook**

– **ACT Math Workbook**

– **GRE Math Workbook**

– **ISEE Math Workbooks**

– **Common Core Math Workbooks**

–**many Math Education Workbooks**

– **and some Mathematics books …**

As an experienced Math teacher, Mr. Smith employs a variety of formats to help students achieve their goals: He tutors online and in person, he teaches students in large groups, and he provides training materials and textbooks through his website and through Amazon.

You can contact Michael via email at:

info@Mathnotion.com

SSAT Lower Level Math Workbook

SSAT Lower Level Math Workbook reviews all SSAT Lower Level Math topics and provides students with the confidence and math skills they need to succeed on the SSAT Lower Level Math. It is designed to address the needs of SSAT Lower Level test takers who must have a working knowledge of basic Mathematics. This comprehensive workbook with over 2,500 sample questions and 2 complete SSAT Lower Level tests can help you fully prepare for the SSAT Lower Level Math test. It provides you with an in-depth focus on the math portion of the exam, helping you master the math skills that students find the most troublesome. This is an incredibly useful tool for those who want to review all topics being covered on the SSAT Lower Level Math test.

SSAT Lower Level Math Workbook contains many exciting features to help you prepare for the SSAT Lower Level Math test, including:

- Content 100% aligned with the 2019-2020 SSAT Lower Level test
- Provided and tested by SSAT Lower Level Math test experts
- Dynamic design and easy-to-follow activities
- A fun, interactive and concrete learning process
- Targeted, skill-building practices
- Complete coverage of all SSAT Lower Level Math topics which you will be tested
- 2 full-length practice tests (featuring new question types) with detailed answers.

The only prep book you will ever need to ace the SSAT Lower Level Math Test!

WWW.MathNotion.COM

… So Much More Online!

✓ FREE Math Lessons

✓ More Math Learning Books!

✓ Mathematics Worksheets

✓ Online Math Tutors

For a PDF Version of This Book

Please Visit WWW.MathNotion.com

Contents

Chapter 1: Place Values and Number Sense

Topics that you'll learn in this chapter:

- ✓ Place Values

- ✓ Compare Numbers

- ✓ Numbers in Word

- ✓ Roman Numerals

- ✓ Rounding

- ✓ Odd or Even

- ✓ Pattern

- ✓ Growing Pattern

Place Values

✍ Write numbers in expanded form.

1) Seventy–one   ___ + ___

2) eighty–five   ___ + ___

3) twenty–three   ___ + ___

4) fifty–four   ___ + ___

5) Ninety–nine   ___ + ___

✍ Circle the correct choice.

6) The 4 in 94 is in the

                Ones place   tens place   hundreds place

7) The 8 in 84 is in the

                Ones place   tens place   hundreds place

8) The 6 in 672 is in the

                Ones place   tens place   hundreds place

9) The 2 in 921 is in the

                Ones place   tens place   hundreds place

10) The 7 in 157 is in the

                Ones place   tens place   hundreds place

Comparing and Ordering Numbers

✍ Use less than, equal to or greater than.

1) 42 _____ 46

2) 89 _____ 79

3) 59 _____ 55

4) 96 _____ 92

5) 89 _____ 89

6) 69 _____ 63

7) 99 _____ 89

8) 38 _____ 25

9) 44 _____ 44

10) 89 _____ 98

11) 16 _____ 26

12) 79 _____ 68

13) 48 _____ 55

14) 13 _____ 31

✍ Order each set numbers from least to greatest.

15) – 15, – 19, 25, – 16, 1   ___, ___, ___, ___, ___, ___

16) 18, –26, 8, – 9, 3   ___, ___, ___, ___, ___, ___

17) 26, – 46, 30, 0, – 26   ___, ___, ___, ___, ___, ___

18) 16, – 86, 0, – 16, 77, –65   ___, ___, ___, ___, ___, ___

19) –20, –81, 80, –36, –69, –49   ___, ___, ___, ___, ___, ___

20) 99, 15, 49, 18, 89, 20   ___, ___, ___, ___, ___, ___

21) 89, 19, 29, 18, 39, 27   ___, ___, ___, ___, ___, ___

Write Numbers in Words

✍ Write each number in words.

1) 456 _____

2) 907 _____

3) 740 _____

4) 132 _____

5) 535 _____

6) 831 _____

7) 2,117 _____

8) 1,578 _____

9) 4,521 _____

10) 5,787 _____

11) 6,672 _____

12) 8,490 _____

13) 3,247 _____

14) 9,019 _____

15) 10,561 _____

Roman Numerals

✍ Write in Romans numerals.

1	I	11	XI	21	XXI
2	II	12	XII	22	XXII
3	III	13	XIII	23	XXIII
4	IV	14	XIV	24	XXIV
5	V	15	XV	25	XXV
6	VI	16	XVI	26	XXVI
7	VII	17	XVII	27	XXVII
8	VIII	18	XVIII	28	XXVIII
9	IX	19	XIX	29	XXIX
10	X	20	XX	30	XXX

1) 13 _____

2) 26 _____

3) 23 _____

4) 19 _____

5) 25 _____

6) 1 8 _____

7) 1 4 _____

8) 9 _____

9) 17 _____

10) 34 _____

11) Add 8 + 13 and write in Roman numerals. _____

12) Subtract 22 – 9 and write in Roman numerals. _____

Rounding Numbers

Round each number to the underlined place value.

1) 2,<u>8</u>82

2) 4,<u>9</u>85

3) 45<u>6</u>3

4) 4,2<u>8</u>1

5) 9,3<u>5</u>6

6) 2,3<u>6</u>4

7) 6,<u>2</u>09

8) 1,3<u>5</u>6

9) 7,<u>3</u>71

10) 8,9<u>2</u>3

11) 5,5<u>4</u>9

12) <u>8</u>,246

13) 10,4<u>6</u>2

14) 2,<u>6</u>98

15) 1,<u>2</u>50

16) 7,<u>6</u>45

17) 9,4<u>9</u>6

18) 5,4<u>3</u>9

19) 8,5<u>9</u>3

20) 11,<u>9</u>39

21) 1<u>9</u>,802

22) 15,4<u>5</u>5

23) 26,<u>8</u>45

24) 9,7<u>1</u>9

Odd or Even

✎ Identify whether each number is even or odd.

1) 28 _____

2) 23 _____

3) 25 _____

4) 15 _____

5) 55 _____

6) 88 _____

7) 42 _____

8) 97 _____

9) 72 _____

10) 60 _____

11) 33 _____

12) 101 _____

✎ Circle the even number in each group.

13) 12, 21, 47, 63, 9, 53

14) 19, 17, 107, 43, 35, 48

15) 29, 37, 64, 57, 65, 99

16) 77, 18, 89, 67, 27, 83

✎ Circle the odd number in each group.

17) 42, 24, 22, 64, 93, 98

18) 18, 26, 20, 44, 66, 75

19) 48, 82, 13, 98, 64, 56

20) 97, 52, 58, 46, 38, 102

Repeating Pattern

✍ Circle the picture that comes next in each picture pattern.

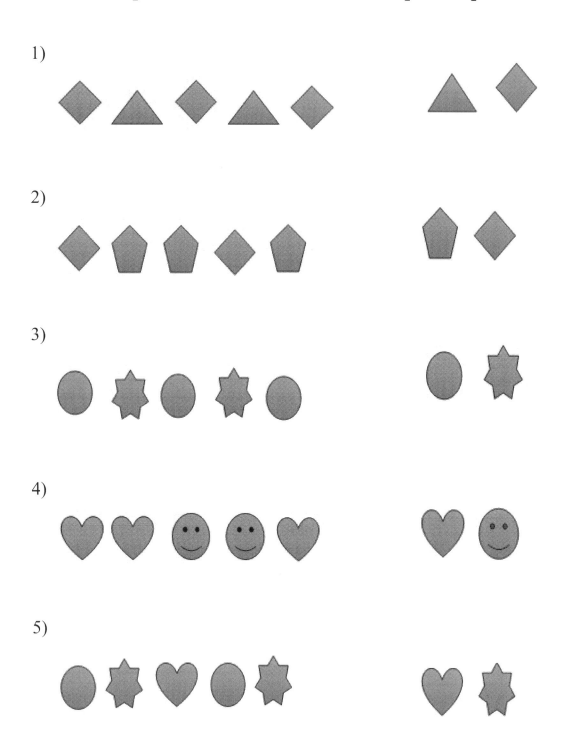

1)

2)

3)

4)

5)

Growing Patterns

✎ Draw the picture that comes next in each growing pattern.

1)

2)

3)

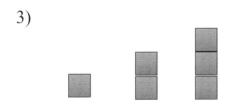

4)

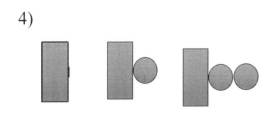

5)

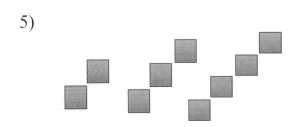

Patterns: Numbers

✎ Write the numbers that come next.

1) 3, 6, 9, 12,   _____, _____, _____, _____

2) 5, 10, 15, 20,   _____, _____, _____, _____

3) 2, 6, 10, 14,   _____, _____, _____, _____

4) 12, 22, 32, 42,   _____, _____, _____, _____

5) 7, 14, 21, 28,   _____, _____, _____, _____

6) 10, 18, 26, 34, 42,   _____, _____, _____, _____

✎ Write the next three numbers in each counting sequence.

1) –41, –29, –17, _____, _____, _____, _____

2) 652, 637, 622, _____, _____, _____, _____

3) 15, 25, _____, _____, 55, _____

4) 25, 33, _____, _____, _____

5) 77, 66, _____, _____, _____

6) 82, 69, 56, _____, _____, _____

7) 256, 224, 192, _____, _____, _____

8) What are the next three numbers in this counting sequence?

   2350, 2450, 2550, _____, _____, _____

9) What is the sixth number in this counting sequence?

                    7, 15, 23, _____

Answers of Worksheets – Chapter 1

Place Values

1) 70 + 1

2) 80 + 5

3) 20 + 3

4) 50 + 4

5) 90 + 9

6) ones place

7) tens place

8) hundreds place

9) tens place

10) one place

Comparing and Ordering Numbers

1) 42 less than 46

2) 89 greater than 79

3) 59 greater than 55

4) 96 greater than 92

5) 89 equals to 89

6) 69 greater than 63

7) 99 greater than 89

8) 38 greater than 25

9) 44 equals to 44

10) 89 less than 98

11) 16 less than 26

12) 79 greater than 68

13) 48 less than 55

14) 13 less than 31

15) –19, –16, –15, 1, 25

16) –26, –9, 3, 8, 18

17) –46, –26, 0, 26, 30

18) –86, –65, –16, 0, 16, 77

19) –81, –69, –49, –35, –20, 80

20) 15, 18, 20, 49, 89, 99

21) 18, 19, 27, 29, 39, 89

Word Names for Numbers

1) four hundred fifty-six

2) nine hundred seven

3) seven hundred forty

4) one hundred thirty-two

5) five hundred thirty -five

6) eight hundred thirty- one

7) two thousand, one hundred seventeen

8) one thousand, five hundred seventy-eight

9) four thousand, five hundred twenty-one

10) five thousand, seven hundred eighty-seven

11) sex thousand, six hundred seventy-two

12) eight thousand, four hundred ninety

13) three thousand, two hundred forty-seven

14) nine thousand, nineteen

15) ten thousand, five hundred sixty-one

Roman Numerals

1) XIII

2) XXVI

3) XXIII

4) XIX

5) XXV

6) XVIII

7) XIV

8) IX

9) XVII

10) XXXIV

11) XXI

12) XIII

Rounding Numbers

1) 2,900

2) 5,000

3) 4,560

4) 4,280

5) 9,360

6) 2,360

7) 6,200

8) 1,360

9) 7,400

10) 8,920

11) 5,550

12) 8,000

13) 10,460   16) 7,600   19) 8,590   22) 15,460

14) 2,700   17) 9,500   20) 11,900   23) 26,800

15) 1,300   18) 5,440   21) 20,000   24) 9,720

Odd or Even

1) even   6) even   11) odd   16) 18

2) odd   7) even   12) odd   17) 93

3) odd   8) odd   13) 12   18) 75

4) odd   9) even   14) 48   19) 13

5) odd   10) even   15) 64   20) 97

Repeating pattern

1)   2)   3)

4)   5)

Growing patterns

1)   2)    3)

4)    5)

Patterns: Numbers

1) 3, 6, 9, 12, 15, 18, 21, 24   4) 12, 22, 32, 42, 52, 62, 72, 82

2) 5, 10, 15, 20, 25, 30, 35, 40   5) 7, 14, 21, 28, 35, 42, 49, 56

3) 2, 6, 10, 14, 18, 22, 26, 30   6) 10, 18, 26, 34, 42, 50, 58, 66

Patterns

1) –5, 7, 19, 31   4) 41–49–57   7) 160,128, 96

2) 607, 592, 577,562   5) 55–44–33   8) 2650–2750–2850

3) 15–25–35–45–55–65   6) 43,30,17   9) 31

Chapter 2: Whole Number Operations

Topics that you'll learn in this chapter:

✓ Adding Whole Numbers

✓ Subtracting Whole Numbers

✓ Multiplying Whole Numbers

✓ Dividing Hundreds

✓ Long Division by One Digit

✓ Division with Remainders

✓ Rounding Whole Numbers

✓ Whole Number Estimation

Adding Whole Numbers

✏️ Add.

1)
$$\begin{array}{r} 4{,}456 \\ +\ 7{,}987 \\ \hline \end{array}$$

4)
$$\begin{array}{r} 4{,}379 \\ +9{,}480 \\ \hline \end{array}$$

2)
$$\begin{array}{r} 5{,}376 \\ +\ 2{,}588 \\ \hline \end{array}$$

5)
$$\begin{array}{r} 7{,}768 \\ +4{,}384 \\ \hline \end{array}$$

3)
$$\begin{array}{r} 4{,}699 \\ +\ 2{,}552 \\ \hline \end{array}$$

6)
$$\begin{array}{r} 6{,}069 \\ +\ 2{,}099 \\ \hline \end{array}$$

✏️ Find the missing numbers.

7) $2{,}265 + \underline{} = 2{,}365$

10) $608 + \underline{} = 1{,}998$

8) $650 + 1{,}200 = \underline{}$

11) $\underline{} + 551 = 4{,}561$

9) $2{,}500 + \underline{} = 6{,}900$

12) $\underline{} + 1{,}890 = 3{,}951$

13) David sells gems. He finds a diamond in Istanbul and buys it for $3,879. Then, he flies to Cairo and purchases a bigger diamond for the bargain price of $8,156. How much does David spend on the two diamonds?

_____

Subtracting Whole Numbers

✍ Subtract.

1) $\begin{array}{r} 8{,}639 \\ -7{,}162 \\ \hline \end{array}$

4) $\begin{array}{r} 7{,}056 \\ -4{,}009 \\ \hline \end{array}$

2) $\begin{array}{r} 4{,}267 \\ -1{,}448 \\ \hline \end{array}$

5) $\begin{array}{r} 9{,}115 \\ -7{,}956 \\ \hline \end{array}$

3) $\begin{array}{r} 7{,}651 \\ -4{,}913 \\ \hline \end{array}$

6) $\begin{array}{r} 3{,}001 \\ -1{,}869 \\ \hline \end{array}$

✍ Find the missing number.

7) $4{,}560 - \underline{\quad} = 2{,}582$

10) $3{,}400 - \underline{\quad} = 1{,}698$

8) $8{,}512 - \underline{\quad} = 3{,}569$

11) $8{,}642 - 6{,}987 = \underline{\quad}$

9) $7{,}243 - 1{,}875 = \underline{\quad}$

12) $7{,}410 - 4{,}568 = \underline{\quad}$

13) Jackson had $5,437 invested in the stock market until he lost $3,891 on those investments. How much money does he have in the stock market now?

_____

Multiplying Whole Numbers

✍ Find the answers.

1)
$$\begin{array}{r} 1100 \\ \times\ 22 \\ \hline \\ \hline \end{array}$$

7)
$$\begin{array}{r} 3129 \\ \times 24 \\ \hline \\ \hline \end{array}$$

2)
$$\begin{array}{r} 4100 \\ \times 15 \\ \hline \\ \hline \end{array}$$

8)
$$\begin{array}{r} 9510 \\ \times 23 \\ \hline \\ \hline \end{array}$$

3)
$$\begin{array}{r} 7960 \\ \times 2 \\ \hline \\ \hline \end{array}$$

9)
$$\begin{array}{r} 3213 \\ \times\ 65 \\ \hline \\ \hline \end{array}$$

4)
$$\begin{array}{r} 6000 \\ \times 4 \\ \hline \\ \hline \end{array}$$

10)
$$\begin{array}{r} 5400 \\ \times\ 17 \\ \hline \\ \hline \end{array}$$

5)
$$\begin{array}{r} 4500 \\ \times 2 \\ \hline \\ \hline \end{array}$$

11)
$$\begin{array}{r} 3700 \\ \times\ 11 \\ \hline \\ \hline \end{array}$$

6)
$$\begin{array}{r} 1400 \\ \times 20 \\ \hline \\ \hline \end{array}$$

12)
$$\begin{array}{r} 9000 \\ \times\ 33 \\ \hline \\ \hline \end{array}$$

Dividing Hundreds

✍Find answers.

1) $2000 \div 200$

2) $1600 \div 20$

3) $900 \div 100$

4) $3,200 \div 800$

5) $4,800 \div 800$

6) $900 \div 300$

7) $2,400 \div 800$

8) $4,500 \div 900$

9) $6,800 \div 200$

10) $10,000 \div 200$

11) $8,100 \div 300$

12) $8,000 \div 500$

13) $1,200 \div 200$

14) $6,600 \div 600$

15) $7,200 \div 600$

16) $1,800 \div 200$

17) $27,000 \div 900$

18) $9,900 \div 300$

19) $7,200 \div 100$

20) $9,000 \div 120$

21) $9,000 \div 3,000$

22) $16,000 \div 40$

23) $210 \div 30$

24) $560 \div 70$

Long Division by Two Digit

✎ Find the quotient.

1) $16\overline{)512}$

2) $12\overline{)816}$

3) $24\overline{)672}$

4) $28\overline{)364}$

5) $34\overline{)578}$

6) $36\overline{)324}$

7) $21\overline{)651}$

8) $42\overline{)2,142}$

9) $65\overline{)1,300}$

10) $45\overline{)1,620}$

11) $63\overline{)2,961}$

12) $50\overline{)2,400}$

13) $27\overline{)2,457}$

14) $67\overline{)7,303}$

15) $93\overline{)4,092}$

16) $76\overline{)6,156}$

17) $70\overline{)12,880}$

18) $18\overline{)11,088}$

Division with Remainders

✎ Find the quotient with remainder.

1) $12\overline{)613}$

2) $15\overline{)2,579}$

3) $23\overline{)3,923}$

4) $81\overline{)3,566}$

5) $38\overline{)6,996}$

6) $75\overline{)8,009}$

7) $59\overline{)7,512}$

8) $85\overline{)11,264}$

9) $45\overline{)7,335}$

10) $88\overline{)12,589}$

11) $36\overline{)9,564}$

12) $60\overline{)36,947}$

13) $78\overline{)6,298}$

14) $95\overline{)37,456}$

Rounding Whole Numbers

✍ Round each number to the underlined place value.

1) 5,9<u>4</u>4

2) 7,<u>5</u>64

3) 7,7<u>7</u>4

4) 3,4<u>8</u>6

5) 6,6<u>7</u>5

6) 1,1<u>5</u>4

7) 4,<u>6</u>04

8) 10,5<u>5</u>9

9) 9,<u>4</u>74

10) 2,8<u>1</u>5

11) 3,9<u>4</u>8

12) 10,<u>2</u>49

13) <u>4</u>,563

14) 9,6<u>8</u>5

15) 4,4<u>3</u>0

16) 1,<u>6</u>86

17) 3,<u>6</u>50

18) 14,<u>0</u>50

19) <u>7</u>,222

20) 2,5<u>3</u>5

21) 11,<u>9</u>65

22) 15,4<u>5</u>5

23) 26,0<u>2</u>5

24) 27,5<u>7</u>9

25) 6,<u>4</u>01

26) 4,1<u>2</u>3

27) 2,<u>8</u>95

Whole Number Estimation

✎ Estimate the sum by rounding each added to the nearest ten.

1) 965 + 485

5) 2,585 + 5,682

2) 1,956 + 2,745

6) 5,754 + 8,386

3) 5,424 + 3,562

7) 4,528 + 5,324

4) 2,743 + 8,246

8) 8,755 + 3,155

9) $\begin{array}{r} 2,864 \\ + 9,547 \\ \hline \end{array}$

12) $\begin{array}{r} 5,379 \\ + 7,445 \\ \hline \end{array}$

10) $\begin{array}{r} 7,531 \\ + 8,765 \\ \hline \end{array}$

13) $\begin{array}{r} 3,168 \\ + 5,025 \\ \hline \end{array}$

11) $\begin{array}{r} 7,523 \\ + 2,388 \\ \hline \end{array}$

14) $\begin{array}{r} 2,270 \\ + 4,129 \\ \hline \end{array}$

Answers of Worksheets – Chapter 2

Adding Whole Numbers

1) 12,443	6) 8,168	11) 4,010
2) 7,964	7) 100	12) 2,061
3) 7,251	8) 1,850	13) $12,035
4) 13,859	9) 4,400	
5) 12,152	10) 13,90	

Subtracting Whole Numbers

1) 1,477	6) 1,132	11) 1,655
2) 2,819	7) 1,978	12) 2,842
3) 2,738	8) 4,943	13) 1,546
4) 3,047	9) 5,368	
5) 1,159	10) 1,702	

Multiplying Whole Numbers

1) 24,200	5) 9,000	9) 208,845
2) 61,500	6) 28,000	10) 91,800
3) 15,920	7) 75,096	11) 40,700
4) 24,000	8) 218,730	12) 297,000

Dividing Whole Numbers

1) 10	7) 3	13) 6	19) 75
2) 80	8) 5	14) 11	20) 75
3) 9	9) 34	15) 12	21) 3
4) 4	10) 50	16) 9	22) 400
5) 6	11) 27	17) 30	23) 7
6) 3	12) 16	18) 33	24) 8

Long Division by One Digit

1) 32	5) 17	9) 20	13) 91
2) 68	6) 9	10) 36	14) 109
3) 28	7) 31	11) 47	15) 44
4) 13	8) 51	12) 48	16) 81

17) 184   18) 616

Division with Remainders

1) 51 R1   6) 106 R59   11) 265 R24

2) 171 R14   7) 127 R19   12) 615 R47

3) 170 R13   8) 132 R44   13) 80 R58

4) 44 R2   9) 163 R0   14) 394 R26

5) 184 R4   10) 143 R5

Rounding Whole Numbers

1) 5,900   10) 2,820   19) 7,000

2) 7,600   11) 3,950   20) 2,540

3) 7,770   12) 10,200   21) 12,000

4) 3,490   13) 5,000   22) 15460

5) 6,680   14) 9,690   23) 26030

6) 1,150   15) 4,400   24) 27,580

7) 4,600   16) 1,700   25) 6,400

8) 10,560   17) 3,700   26) 4,120

9) 9,500   18) 14,100   27) 2,900

Whole Number Estimation

1) 1,460   6) 14,140   11) 9,910

2) 4,710   7) 9,850   12) 12,830

3) 8,980   8) 11,920   13) 8,200

4) 10,990   9) 12,410   14) 6,400

5) 8,270   10) 16,300

Chapter 3: Number Theory

Topics that you'll learn in this chapter:

- ✓ Factoring Numbers

- ✓ Prime Factorization

- ✓ Divisibility Rules

- ✓ Greatest Common Factor

- ✓ Least Common Multiple

Factoring Numbers

List all positive factors of each number.

1) 14	6) 75	11) 39
2) 18	7) 66	12) 35
3) 32	8) 60	13) 54
4) 42	9) 38	14) 22
5) 24	10) 52	15) 84

List the prime factorization for each number.

16) 12	19) 45	22) 49
17) 36	20) 50	23) 85
18) 22	21) 64	24) 94

Prime Factorization

Factor the following numbers to their prime factors.

1) 15	9) 66	17) 91
2) 22	10) 36	18) 30
3) 9	11) 14	19) 8
4) 24	12) 56	20) 12
5) 16	13) 52	21) 63
6) 34	14) 70	22) 33
7) 28	15) 84	23) 35
8) 26	16) 22	24) 54

Divisibility Rules

✍ Use the divisibility rules to underline the factors of the number.

1) 10   2 3 4 5 6 7 8 9 10

2) 12   2 3 4 5 6 7 8 9 10

3) 24   2 3 4 5 6 7 8 9 10

4) 15   2 3 4 5 6 7 8 9 10

5) 30   2 3 4 5 6 7 8 9 10

6) 5   2 3 4 5 6 7 8 9 10

7) 32   2 3 4 5 6 7 8 9 10

8) 48   2 3 4 5 6 7 8 9 10

9) 16   2 3 4 5 6 7 8 9 10

10) 25   2 3 4 5 6 7 8 9 10

11) 35   2 3 4 5 6 7 8 9 10

12) 49   2 3 4 5 6 7 8 9 10

Greatest Common Factor

✎ Find the GCF for each number pair.

1) 20, 30	9) 32, 4	17) 65, 49
2) 6, 14	10) 17, 21	18) 50, 45
3) 5, 35	11) 16, 2	19) 98, 10
4) 48, 12	12) 49, 7	20) 50, 25
5) 17, 13	13) 32, 36	21) 110, 40
6) 33, 27	14) 80, 70	22) 36, 12
7) 12, 15	15) 82, 42	23) 24, 25
8) 34, 8	16) 80, 35	24) 15, 60

Least Common Multiple

✎ Find the LCM for each number pair.

1) 2, 12	9) 11, 10	17) 12, 4, 24
2) 3, 18	10) 9, 36	18) 11, 7, 9
3) 16, 4	11) 19, 7	19) 5, 6, 30
4) 15, 20	12) 7, 9	20) 8, 32, 5
5) 6, 18	13) 30, 6	21) 4, 8, 6
6) 12, 6	14) 8, 2	22) 12, 8, 96
7) 25, 12	15) 20, 10, 15	23) 5, 15, 25
8) 8, 7	16) 12, 6, 18	24) 24, 2, 5

Answers of Worksheets – Chapter 3

Factoring Numbers

1) 1, 2, 7, 14

2) 1, 2, 3, 6, 9, 18

3) 1, 2, 4, 8, 16, 32

4) 1, 2, 3, 6, 7, 14, 21, 42

5) 1, 2, 3, 4, 6, 8, 12, 24

6) 1, 3, 5, 15, 25, 75

7) 1, 2, 3, 6, 11, 22, 33, 66

8) 1, 2, 3, 4, 5, 6, 10, 12, 15, 20, 30, 60

9) 1, 2, 19, 38

10) 1, 2, 4, 13, 26, 52

11) 1, 3, 13, 39

12) 1, 5, 7, 35

13) 1, 2, 3, 6, 9, 18, 27, 54

14) 1, 2, 11, 22

15) 1, 2, 3, 4, 6, 7, 12, 14, 21, 28, 42, 84

16) $2 \times 2 \times 3$

17) $2 \times 2 \times 3 \times 3$

18) 2×11

19) $3 \times 3 \times 5$

20) $2 \times 5 \times 5$

21) $2 \times 2 \times 2 \times 2 \times 2$

22) 7×7

23) $5 \times 1 7$

24) 2×47

Prime Factorization

1) 3. 5

2) 2. 11

3) 3. 3

4) 2. 2. 2. 3

5) 2. 2. 2. 2

6) 2. 17

7) 2. 2. 7

8) 2. 13

9) 2. 3. 11

10) 2. 2. 3. 3

11) 2. 7

12) 2. 2. 2. 7

13) 2. 2. 13

14) 2. 5. 7

15) 2. 2. 3.7

16) 2. 11

17) 7.13

18) 2. 3. 5

19) 2. 2. 2

20) 2. 2. 3

21) 3. 3. 7

22) 3. 11

23) 5. 7

24) 2. 3. 3. 3

Divisibility Rules

1) 10   2 3 4 5 6 7 8 9 10

2) 12   2 3 4 5 6 7 8 9 10

3) 24   2 3 4 5 6 7 8 9 10

4) 15   2 3 4 5 6 7 8 9 10

5) 30   2 3 4 5 6 7 8 9 10

6) 5   2 3 4 5 6 7 8 9 10

7) 32   2 3 4 5 6 7 8 9 10

8) 48   2 3 4 5 6 7 8 9 10

9) 16   <u>2</u>   3   <u>4</u>   5   6   7   <u>8</u>   9   10

10) 25   2   3   4   <u>5</u>   6   7   8   9   10

11) 35   2   3   4   <u>5</u>   6   <u>7</u>   8   9   10

12) 49   2   3   4   5   6   <u>7</u>   8   9   10

Greatest Common Factor

1) 10	7) 3	13) 4	19) 2
2) 2	8) 2	14) 10	20) 25
3) 5	9) 4	15) 2	21) 10
4) 12	10) 1	16) 5	22) 12
5) 1	11) 2	17) 1	23) 1
6) 3	12) 7	18) 5	24) 15

Least Common Multiple

1) 14	7) 300	13) 30	19) 30
2) 18	8) 56	14) 8	20) 160
3) 16	9) 110	15) 60	21) 24
4) 60	10) 36	16) 36	22) 96
5) 18	11) 133	17) 24	23) 75
6) 12	12) 63	18) 693	24) 120

Chapter 4: Fractions and Mixed Numbers

Topics that you'll learn in this chapter:

- ✓ Simplifying Fractions

- ✓ Add and Subtract Fractions with Like Denominators

- ✓ Compare Fractions with Like Denominators

- ✓ More than two Fractions with Like Denominators

- ✓ Add and Subtract Fractions with Unlike Denominators

- ✓ Ordering Fractions

- ✓ Add and Subtract Fractions with Denominators of 10, 100, and 1000

- ✓ Fractions to Mixed Numbers

- ✓ Mixed Numbers to Fractions

- ✓ Add and Subtract Mixed Numbers with Like Denominators

Simplifying Fractions

✎ Simplify the fractions.

1) $\dfrac{33}{63}$

2) $\dfrac{4}{10}$

3) $\dfrac{15}{20}$

4) $\dfrac{5}{30}$

5) $\dfrac{13}{26}$

6) $\dfrac{7}{49}$

7) $\dfrac{6}{21}$

8) $\dfrac{15}{45}$

9) $\dfrac{8}{10}$

10) $\dfrac{8}{56}$

11) $\dfrac{14}{42}$

12) $\dfrac{30}{20}$

13) $\dfrac{30}{42}$

14) $\dfrac{21}{28}$

15) $\dfrac{13}{65}$

16) $\dfrac{25}{40}$

17) $\dfrac{12}{32}$

18) $\dfrac{24}{64}$

19) $\dfrac{11}{99}$

20) $\dfrac{36}{48}$

21) $\dfrac{8}{72}$

22) $\dfrac{17}{34}$

Like Denominators

✎ Add fractions.

1) $\dfrac{2}{3}+\dfrac{1}{3}$

2) $\dfrac{2}{9}+\dfrac{7}{9}$

3) $\dfrac{5}{8}+\dfrac{6}{8}$

4) $\dfrac{1}{6}+\dfrac{3}{6}$

5) $\dfrac{4}{11}+\dfrac{3}{11}$

6) $\dfrac{3}{12}+\dfrac{2}{12}$

7) $\dfrac{1}{7}+\dfrac{3}{7}$

8) $\dfrac{5}{15}+\dfrac{7}{15}$

9) $\dfrac{5}{19}+\dfrac{10}{19}$

10) $\dfrac{4}{7}+\dfrac{4}{7}$

11) $\dfrac{3}{16}+\dfrac{7}{16}$

12) $\dfrac{8}{15}+\dfrac{10}{15}$

13) $\dfrac{11}{17}+\dfrac{6}{17}$

14) $\dfrac{7}{18}+\dfrac{5}{18}$

15) $\dfrac{7}{13}+\dfrac{1}{13}$

16) $\dfrac{10}{24}+\dfrac{11}{24}$

17) $\dfrac{12}{34}+\dfrac{11}{34}$

18) $\dfrac{4}{11}+\dfrac{5}{11}$

19) $\dfrac{12}{41}+\dfrac{11}{41}$

20) $\dfrac{8}{38}+\dfrac{15}{38}$

21) $\dfrac{17}{39}+\dfrac{2}{39}$

22) $\dfrac{7}{13}+\dfrac{6}{13}$

23) $\dfrac{4}{9}+\dfrac{2}{9}$

24) $\dfrac{5}{23}+\dfrac{2}{23}$

25) $\dfrac{8}{10}+\dfrac{1}{10}$

26) $\dfrac{7}{13}+\dfrac{1}{13}$

27) $\dfrac{4}{18}+\dfrac{3}{18}$

28) $\dfrac{9}{21}+\dfrac{12}{21}$

29) $\dfrac{4}{11}+\dfrac{4}{11}$

30) $\dfrac{12}{35}+\dfrac{5}{35}$

✐Subtract fractions.

1) $\dfrac{5}{7} - \dfrac{2}{7}$

2) $\dfrac{4}{5} - \dfrac{2}{5}$

3) $\dfrac{10}{13} - \dfrac{4}{13}$

4) $\dfrac{7}{9} - \dfrac{2}{9}$

5) $\dfrac{5}{10} - \dfrac{3}{10}$

6) $\dfrac{4}{7} - \dfrac{3}{7}$

7) $\dfrac{7}{17} - \dfrac{5}{17}$

8) $\dfrac{14}{15} - \dfrac{2}{15}$

9) $\dfrac{8}{21} - \dfrac{5}{21}$

10) $\dfrac{10}{12} - \dfrac{8}{12}$

11) $\dfrac{10}{14} - \dfrac{2}{14}$

12) $\dfrac{11}{21} - \dfrac{1}{21}$

13) $\dfrac{12}{29} - \dfrac{11}{29}$

14) $\dfrac{5}{36} - \dfrac{1}{36}$

15) $\dfrac{25}{27} - \dfrac{15}{27}$

16) $\dfrac{22}{45} - \dfrac{12}{45}$

17) $\dfrac{31}{39} - \dfrac{26}{39}$

18) $\dfrac{14}{26} - \dfrac{13}{26}$

19) $\dfrac{35}{47} - \dfrac{15}{47}$

20) $\dfrac{29}{34} - \dfrac{19}{34}$

21) $\dfrac{21}{38} - \dfrac{9}{38}$

22) $\dfrac{3}{9} - \dfrac{2}{9}$

23) $\dfrac{5}{6} - \dfrac{3}{6}$

24) $\dfrac{3}{5} - \dfrac{2}{5}$

25) $\dfrac{7}{14} - \dfrac{2}{14}$

26) $\dfrac{6}{42} - \dfrac{3}{42}$

27) $\dfrac{4}{23} - \dfrac{1}{23}$

28) $\dfrac{5}{16} - \dfrac{4}{16}$

29) $\dfrac{15}{55} - \dfrac{2}{55}$

30) $\dfrac{10}{27} - \dfrac{7}{27}$

Compare Fractions with Like Denominators

✎ Evaluate and compare. Write < or > or =.

1) $\dfrac{1}{4} + \dfrac{2}{4} \underline{} \dfrac{1}{4}$

9) $\dfrac{15}{19} - \dfrac{3}{19} \underline{} \dfrac{15}{19}$

2) $\dfrac{4}{5} + \dfrac{1}{5} \underline{} \dfrac{3}{5}$

10) $\dfrac{18}{22} + \dfrac{4}{22} \underline{} \dfrac{17}{22}$

3) $\dfrac{5}{8} - \dfrac{3}{8} \underline{} \dfrac{6}{8}$

11) $\dfrac{10}{18} - \dfrac{4}{18} \underline{} \dfrac{15}{18}$

4) $\dfrac{8}{12} + \dfrac{7}{12} \underline{} \dfrac{4}{12}$

12) $\dfrac{27}{45} - \dfrac{11}{45} \underline{} \dfrac{20}{45}$

5) $\dfrac{4}{7} - \dfrac{3}{7} \underline{} \dfrac{4}{7}$

13) $\dfrac{25}{30} + \dfrac{5}{30} \underline{} \dfrac{18}{30}$

6) $\dfrac{9}{13} - \dfrac{4}{13} \underline{} \dfrac{3}{13}$

14) $\dfrac{20}{25} - \dfrac{3}{25} \underline{} \dfrac{9}{25}$

7) $\dfrac{3}{10} + \dfrac{1}{10} \underline{} \dfrac{1}{10}$

15) $\dfrac{45}{49} - \dfrac{25}{49} \underline{} \dfrac{37}{49}$

8) $\dfrac{12}{10} + \dfrac{2}{10} \underline{} \dfrac{7}{10}$

16) $\dfrac{32}{39} + \dfrac{12}{39} \underline{} \dfrac{18}{39}$

More Than Two Fractions with Like Denominators

✎ Add fractions.

1) $\frac{4}{8} + \frac{3}{8} + \frac{1}{8}$

2) $\frac{2}{5} + \frac{2}{5} + \frac{1}{5}$

3) $\frac{3}{10} + \frac{1}{10} + \frac{3}{10}$

4) $\frac{2}{7} + \frac{2}{7} + \frac{2}{7}$

5) $\frac{5}{14} + \frac{3}{14} + \frac{4}{14}$

6) $\frac{5}{21} + \frac{1}{21} + \frac{4}{21}$

7) $\frac{4}{11} + \frac{2}{11} + \frac{1}{11}$

8) $\frac{6}{19} + \frac{5}{19} + \frac{4}{19}$

9) $\frac{15}{31} + \frac{1}{31} + \frac{7}{31}$

10) $\frac{1}{14} + \frac{5}{14} + \frac{8}{14}$

11) $\frac{3}{25} + \frac{4}{25} + \frac{4}{25}$

12) $\frac{5}{20} + \frac{10}{20} + \frac{6}{20}$

13) $\frac{8}{39} + \frac{7}{39} + \frac{6}{39}$

14) $\frac{9}{29} + \frac{10}{29} + \frac{5}{29}$

15) $\frac{7}{24} + \frac{1}{24} + \frac{3}{24}$

16) $\frac{2}{13} + \frac{7}{13} + \frac{3}{13}$

Unlike Denominators

✎Add fraction.

1) $\frac{1}{5} + \frac{1}{7}$

2) $\frac{3}{8} + \frac{1}{2}$

3) $\frac{3}{4} + \frac{1}{7}$

4) $\frac{1}{6} + \frac{2}{3}$

5) $\frac{2}{9} + \frac{1}{2}$

6) $\frac{3}{4} + \frac{2}{5}$

7) $\frac{16}{15} + \frac{3}{5}$

8) $\frac{3}{11} + \frac{1}{2}$

9) $\frac{3}{6} + \frac{2}{7}$

10) $\frac{1}{3} + \frac{1}{21}$

11) $\frac{2}{8} + \frac{1}{3}$

12) $\frac{5}{36} + \frac{2}{6}$

13) $\frac{3}{16} + \frac{1}{4}$

14) $\frac{5}{4} + \frac{1}{6}$

15) $\frac{1}{8} + \frac{2}{9}$

16) $\frac{2}{9} + \frac{1}{3}$

17) $\frac{3}{2} + \frac{2}{5}$

18) $\frac{2}{7} + \frac{1}{4}$

19) $\frac{1}{4} + \frac{1}{24}$

20) $\frac{13}{32} + \frac{3}{8}$

21) $\frac{3}{13} + \frac{1}{2}$

22) $\frac{2}{22} + \frac{1}{2}$

✎ Subtract fractions.

1) $\dfrac{3}{7} - \dfrac{1}{3}$

2) $\dfrac{3}{5} - \dfrac{1}{4}$

3) $\dfrac{1}{3} - \dfrac{1}{5}$

4) $\dfrac{6}{6} - \dfrac{3}{5}$

5) $\dfrac{3}{3} - \dfrac{3}{21}$

6) $\dfrac{15}{20} - \dfrac{1}{10}$

7) $\dfrac{3}{12} - \dfrac{1}{6}$

8) $\dfrac{8}{9} - \dfrac{2}{3}$

9) $\dfrac{13}{25} - \dfrac{1}{5}$

10) $\dfrac{1}{3} - \dfrac{1}{15}$

11) $\dfrac{4}{5} - \dfrac{2}{7}$

12) $\dfrac{1}{2} - \dfrac{2}{9}$

13) $\dfrac{3}{7} - \dfrac{1}{4}$

14) $\dfrac{5}{3} - \dfrac{1}{4}$

15) $\dfrac{1}{7} - \dfrac{2}{28}$

16) $\dfrac{1}{5} - \dfrac{6}{35}$

17) $\dfrac{29}{32} - \dfrac{3}{4}$

18) $\dfrac{4}{9} - \dfrac{1}{3}$

19) $\dfrac{13}{44} - \dfrac{2}{11}$

20) $\dfrac{1}{2} - \dfrac{4}{11}$

21) $\dfrac{3}{4} - \dfrac{2}{7}$

22) $\dfrac{4}{5} - \dfrac{1}{8}$

Ordering Fractions

✐ Order the fractions from least to greatest.

1) $\dfrac{1}{4}, \dfrac{1}{6}, \dfrac{1}{7}, \dfrac{1}{2}$ _____, _____, _____, _____

2) $\dfrac{1}{4}, \dfrac{1}{12}, \dfrac{3}{6}, \dfrac{1}{3}$ _____, _____, _____, _____

3) $\dfrac{5}{8}, \dfrac{2}{8}, \dfrac{12}{16}, \dfrac{5}{16}$ _____, _____, _____, _____

4) $\dfrac{2}{3}, \dfrac{5}{6}, \dfrac{3}{4}, \dfrac{7}{12}$ _____, _____, _____, _____

5) $\dfrac{1}{2}, \dfrac{3}{8}, \dfrac{5}{32}, \dfrac{1}{4}$ _____, _____, _____, _____

✐ Order the fractions from greatest to least.

6) $\dfrac{2}{5}, \dfrac{3}{8}, \dfrac{4}{12}, \dfrac{7}{11}$ _____, _____, _____, _____

7) $\dfrac{7}{10}, \dfrac{3}{5}, \dfrac{3}{4}, \dfrac{1}{2}$ _____, _____, _____, _____

8) $\dfrac{5}{7}, \dfrac{1}{5}, \dfrac{4}{12}, \dfrac{2}{3}$ _____, _____, _____, _____

9) $\dfrac{5}{6}, \dfrac{3}{8}, \dfrac{9}{16}, \dfrac{11}{12}$ _____, _____, _____, _____

10) $\dfrac{14}{30}, \dfrac{13}{14}, \dfrac{15}{28}, \dfrac{4}{15}$ _____, _____, _____, _____

Denominators of 10, 100, and 1000

✎ Add fractions.

1) $\dfrac{5}{10} + \dfrac{20}{100}$

2) $\dfrac{5}{10} + \dfrac{40}{100}$

3) $\dfrac{28}{100} + \dfrac{6}{10}$

4) $\dfrac{73}{100} + \dfrac{1}{10}$

5) $\dfrac{43}{100} + \dfrac{1}{10}$

6) $\dfrac{4}{10} + \dfrac{40}{100}$

7) $\dfrac{5}{100} + \dfrac{2}{10}$

8) $\dfrac{20}{100} + \dfrac{8}{10}$

9) $\dfrac{36}{100} + \dfrac{3}{10}$

10) $\dfrac{7}{10} + \dfrac{15}{100}$

11) $\dfrac{5}{10} + \dfrac{50}{100}$

12) $\dfrac{40}{100} + \dfrac{1}{10}$

13) $\dfrac{23}{100} + \dfrac{5}{10}$

14) $\dfrac{11}{100} + \dfrac{7}{10}$

15) $\dfrac{15}{100} + \dfrac{4}{10}$

16) $\dfrac{7}{10} + \dfrac{21}{100}$

17) $\dfrac{35}{100} + \dfrac{3}{10}$

18) $\dfrac{86}{100} + \dfrac{1}{10}$

✎ Subtract fractions.

1) $\dfrac{9}{10} - \dfrac{30}{100}$

2) $\dfrac{4}{10} - \dfrac{17}{100}$

3) $\dfrac{15}{100} - \dfrac{50}{1000}$

4) $\dfrac{85}{100} - \dfrac{150}{1000}$

5) $\dfrac{33}{100} - \dfrac{130}{1000}$

6) $\dfrac{40}{10} - \dfrac{380}{1000}$

7) $\dfrac{80}{100} - \dfrac{660}{1000}$

8) $\dfrac{80}{100} - \dfrac{5}{10}$

9) $\dfrac{460}{1000} - \dfrac{3}{10}$

10) $\dfrac{64}{100} - \dfrac{140}{1000}$

11) $\dfrac{8}{10} - \dfrac{25}{100}$

12) $\dfrac{45}{100} - \dfrac{3}{10}$

13) $\dfrac{40}{100} - \dfrac{2}{10}$

14) $\dfrac{600}{1000} - \dfrac{1}{100}$

15) $\dfrac{600}{1000} - \dfrac{50}{100}$

16) $\dfrac{670}{1000} - \dfrac{4}{10}$

17) $\dfrac{70}{100} - \dfrac{6}{10}$

18) $\dfrac{80}{100} - \dfrac{350}{1000}$

Fractions to Mixed Numbers

✎ Convert fractions to mixed numbers.

1) $\dfrac{7}{4}$

2) $\dfrac{44}{5}$

3) $\dfrac{27}{6}$

4) $\dfrac{22}{10}$

5) $\dfrac{9}{2}$

6) $\dfrac{46}{10}$

7) $\dfrac{28}{8}$

8) $\dfrac{13}{5}$

9) $\dfrac{22}{5}$

10) $\dfrac{16}{10}$

11) $\dfrac{14}{6}$

12) $\dfrac{30}{8}$

13) $\dfrac{11}{2}$

14) $\dfrac{33}{4}$

15) $\dfrac{52}{10}$

16) $\dfrac{14}{3}$

17) $\dfrac{51}{8}$

18) $\dfrac{29}{5}$

19) $\dfrac{19}{6}$

20) $\dfrac{13}{5}$

Mixed Numbers to Fractions

✎ Convert to fraction.

1) $2\frac{2}{7}$

2) $1\frac{3}{5}$

3) $7\frac{1}{4}$

4) $4\frac{4}{7}$

5) $4\frac{1}{4}$

6) $1\frac{3}{7}$

7) $4\frac{4}{9}$

8) $6\frac{9}{10}$

9) $7\frac{5}{6}$

10) $5\frac{10}{11}$

11) $2\frac{9}{20}$

12) $7\frac{2}{7}$

13) $4\frac{3}{5}$

14) $6\frac{1}{6}$

15) $9\frac{3}{4}$

16) $12\frac{2}{5}$

17) $11\frac{3}{7}$

18) $13\frac{6}{7}$

19) $4\frac{6}{7}$

20) $10\frac{2}{3}$

21) $11\frac{1}{5}$

22) $5\frac{2}{7}$

Add and Subtract Mixed Numbers

✎ Add mixed numbers.

1) $2\frac{2}{3} + 7\frac{1}{2}$

2) $5\frac{1}{2} + 5\frac{4}{5}$

3) $7\frac{1}{5} + 3\frac{1}{2}$

4) $5\frac{1}{2} + 4\frac{1}{3}$

5) $5\frac{1}{3} - 2\frac{2}{3}$

6) $8\frac{3}{15} - 3\frac{3}{5}$

7) $8\frac{3}{7} - 4\frac{5}{7}$

8) $4\frac{6}{5} - 1\frac{8}{15}$

9) $6\frac{21}{25} - 2\frac{12}{25}$

10) $4\frac{2}{8} + 4\frac{1}{2}$

11) $2\frac{5}{8} + 3\frac{1}{8}$

12) $3\frac{2}{7} + 5\frac{1}{5}$

13) $9\frac{1}{3} - 4\frac{2}{3}$

14) $1\frac{2}{7} + 4\frac{1}{5}$

15) $1\frac{1}{5} + 3\frac{1}{2}$

16) $5\frac{1}{2} - 2\frac{2}{3}$

17) $\frac{1}{2} + 4\frac{1}{4}$

18) $4\frac{2}{3} + 3\frac{1}{6}$

Answers of Worksheets – Chapter 4

Simplifying Fractions

1) $\frac{11}{21}$

2) $\frac{2}{5}$

3) $\frac{3}{4}$

4) $\frac{1}{6}$

5) $\frac{1}{2}$

6) $\frac{1}{7}$

7) $\frac{2}{7}$

8) $\frac{1}{3}$

9) $\frac{4}{5}$

10) $\frac{1}{7}$

11) $\frac{1}{3}$

12) $\frac{3}{2}$

13) $\frac{5}{7}$

14) $\frac{3}{4}$

15) $\frac{1}{5}$

16) $\frac{5}{8}$

17) $\frac{3}{8}$

18) $\frac{3}{8}$

19) $\frac{1}{9}$

20) $\frac{3}{4}$

21) $\frac{1}{9}$

22) $\frac{1}{2}$

Add Fractions with Like Denominators

1) 1

2) 1

3) $\frac{11}{8}$

4) $\frac{4}{6}$

5) $\frac{7}{11}$

6) $\frac{5}{12}$

7) $\frac{4}{7}$

8) $\frac{12}{15}$

9) $\frac{15}{19}$

10) $\frac{8}{7}$

11) $\frac{10}{16}$

12) $\frac{18}{15}$

13) 1

14) $\frac{12}{18}$

15) $\frac{8}{13}$

16) $\frac{21}{24}$

17) $\frac{23}{34}$

18) $\frac{9}{11}$

19) $\frac{23}{41}$

20) $\frac{23}{38}$

21) $\frac{19}{39}$

22) 1

23) $\frac{6}{9}$

24) $\frac{7}{23}$

25) $\frac{9}{10}$

26) $\frac{8}{13}$

27) $\frac{7}{18}$

28) 1

29) $\frac{8}{11}$

30) $\frac{17}{35}$

Subtract Fractions with Like Denominators

1) $\frac{3}{7}$

2) $\frac{2}{5}$

3) $\frac{6}{13}$

4) $\frac{5}{9}$

5) $\frac{7}{10}$

6) $\frac{1}{7}$

7) $\frac{2}{17}$

8) $\frac{12}{15}$

9) $\frac{3}{21}$

10) $\frac{2}{12}$

11) $\frac{8}{14}$

12) $\frac{9}{21}$

13) $\frac{1}{29}$

14) $\frac{4}{36}$

15) $\frac{10}{27}$

16) $\frac{10}{45}$ 21) $\frac{12}{38}$ 26) $\frac{3}{42}$

17) $\frac{5}{39}$ 22) $\frac{1}{9}$ 27) $\frac{3}{23}$

18) $\frac{1}{26}$ 23) $\frac{2}{6}$ 28) $\frac{1}{16}$

19) $\frac{20}{47}$ 24) $\frac{1}{5}$ 29) $\frac{13}{55}$

20) $\frac{10}{34}$ 25) $\frac{5}{14}$ 30) $\frac{3}{27}$

Compare Fractions with Like Denominators

1) $\frac{3}{4} > \frac{1}{4}$ 7) $\frac{4}{10} > \frac{1}{10}$ 13) $1 > \frac{18}{30}$

2) $1 > \frac{3}{5}$ 8) $\frac{14}{10} > \frac{7}{10}$ 14) $\frac{17}{25} > \frac{9}{25}$

3) $\frac{2}{8} < \frac{6}{8}$ 9) $\frac{12}{19} < \frac{15}{19}$ 15) $\frac{20}{49} < \frac{37}{49}$

4) $\frac{15}{12} > \frac{4}{12}$ 10) $1 > \frac{17}{22}$ 16) $\frac{44}{39} > \frac{18}{39}$

5) $\frac{1}{7} < \frac{4}{7}$ 11) $\frac{6}{18} < \frac{15}{18}$

6) $\frac{5}{13} > \frac{3}{13}$ 12) $\frac{16}{45} < \frac{20}{45}$

More Than Two Fractions with Like Denominators

1) 1   5) $\frac{12}{14}$ 9) $\frac{23}{31}$ 13) $\frac{21}{39}$

2) 1   6) $\frac{10}{21}$ 10) 1   14) $\frac{24}{29}$

3) $\frac{7}{8}$ 7) $\frac{7}{11}$ 11) $\frac{11}{25}$ 15) $\frac{11}{24}$

4) $\frac{6}{7}$ 8) $\frac{16}{19}$ 12) $\frac{21}{20}$ 16) $\frac{12}{13}$

Add fractions with unlike denominators

1) $\frac{12}{35}$ 6) $\frac{23}{20}$ 11) $\frac{7}{12}$ 16) $\frac{5}{9}$

2) $\frac{7}{8}$ 7) $\frac{25}{15}$ 12) $\frac{17}{36}$ 17) $\frac{19}{10}$

3) $\frac{25}{28}$ 8) $\frac{17}{22}$ 13) $\frac{7}{16}$ 18) $\frac{15}{28}$

4) $\frac{5}{6}$ 9) $\frac{11}{14}$ 14) $\frac{17}{12}$ 19) $\frac{7}{24}$

5) $\frac{13}{18}$ 10) $\frac{8}{21}$ 15) $\frac{25}{72}$ 20) $\frac{25}{32}$

21) $\frac{19}{26}$ 22) $\frac{13}{22}$

Subtract fractions with unlike denominators

1) $\frac{2}{21}$ 7) $\frac{1}{12}$ 13) $\frac{5}{28}$ 19) $\frac{5}{44}$

2) $\frac{7}{20}$ 8) $\frac{2}{9}$ 14) $\frac{17}{12}$ 20) $\frac{3}{22}$

3) $\frac{2}{15}$ 9) $\frac{8}{25}$ 15) $\frac{1}{14}$ 21) $\frac{13}{28}$

4) $\frac{2}{5}$ 10) $\frac{4}{15}$ 16) $\frac{1}{35}$ 22) $\frac{27}{40}$

5) $\frac{6}{7}$ 11) $\frac{18}{35}$ 17) $\frac{5}{32}$

6) $\frac{13}{20}$ 12) $\frac{5}{18}$ 18) $\frac{1}{9}$

Ordering Fractions

1) $\frac{1}{7}, \frac{1}{6}, \frac{1}{4}, \frac{1}{2}$ 5) $\frac{5}{32}, \frac{1}{4}, \frac{3}{8}, \frac{1}{2}$ 9) $\frac{11}{12}, \frac{5}{6}, \frac{9}{16}, \frac{3}{8}$

2) $\frac{1}{12}, \frac{1}{4}, \frac{1}{3}, \frac{3}{6},$ 6) $\frac{7}{11}, \frac{2}{5}, \frac{3}{8}, \frac{4}{12}$ 10) $\frac{13}{14}, \frac{15}{28}, \frac{14}{30}, \frac{4}{15}$

3) $\frac{2}{8}, \frac{5}{16}, \frac{5}{8}, \frac{12}{16}$ 7) $\frac{3}{4}, \frac{7}{10}, \frac{3}{5}, \frac{1}{2}$

4) $\frac{7}{12}, \frac{2}{3}, \frac{3}{4}, \frac{5}{6}$ 8) $\frac{5}{7}, \frac{2}{3}, \frac{4}{12}, \frac{1}{5}$

Add fractions with denominators of 10, 100, and 1000

1) $\frac{7}{10}$ 6) $\frac{4}{5}$ 11) 1   16) $\frac{91}{100}$

2) $\frac{9}{10}$ 7) $\frac{1}{4}$ 12) $\frac{1}{2}$ 17) $\frac{13}{20}$

3) $\frac{22}{25}$ 8) 1   13) $\frac{73}{100}$ 18) $\frac{24}{25}$

4) $\frac{83}{100}$ 9) $\frac{33}{50}$ 14) $\frac{81}{100}$

5) $\frac{53}{100}$ 10) $\frac{17}{20}$ 15) $\frac{11}{20}$

Subtract fractions with denominators of 10, 100, and 1000

1) $\frac{3}{5}$ 4) $\frac{7}{10}$ 7) $\frac{7}{50}$ 10) $\frac{1}{2}$

2) $\frac{23}{100}$ 5) $\frac{1}{5}$ 8) $\frac{3}{10}$ 11) $\frac{11}{20}$

3) $\frac{1}{10}$ 6) $\frac{181}{50}$ 9) $\frac{4}{25}$ 12) $\frac{3}{20}$

13) $\frac{1}{5}$ 15) $\frac{1}{10}$ 17) $\frac{1}{10}$

14) $\frac{59}{100}$ 16) $\frac{27}{100}$ 18) $\frac{9}{20}$

Fractions to Mixed Numbers

1) $1\frac{3}{4}$ 6) $4\frac{3}{5}$ 11) $2\frac{1}{3}$ 16) $4\frac{2}{3}$

2) $8\frac{4}{5}$ 7) $3\frac{1}{2}$ 12) $3\frac{3}{4}$ 17) $6\frac{3}{8}$

3) $4\frac{1}{2}$ 8) $2\frac{3}{5}$ 13) $5\frac{1}{2}$ 18) $5\frac{4}{5}$

4) $2\frac{1}{5}$ 9) $4\frac{2}{5}$ 14) $8\frac{1}{4}$ 19) $3\frac{1}{6}$

5) $4\frac{1}{2}$ 10) $1\frac{3}{5}$ 15) $5\frac{1}{5}$ 20) $2\frac{3}{5}$

Mixed Numbers to Fractions

1) $\frac{16}{7}$ 7) $\frac{40}{9}$ 13) $\frac{23}{5}$ 19) $\frac{34}{7}$

2) $\frac{8}{5}$ 8) $\frac{69}{10}$ 14) $\frac{37}{6}$ 20) $\frac{32}{3}$

3) $\frac{29}{4}$ 9) $\frac{47}{6}$ 15) $\frac{39}{4}$ 21) $\frac{56}{5}$

4) $\frac{32}{7}$ 10) $\frac{65}{11}$ 16) $\frac{62}{5}$ 22) $\frac{37}{7}$

5) $\frac{17}{4}$ 11) $\frac{49}{20}$ 17) $\frac{80}{7}$

6) $\frac{10}{7}$ 12) $\frac{51}{7}$ 18) $\frac{97}{7}$

Add and Subtract Mixed Numbers with Like Denominators

1) $10\frac{1}{6}$ 6) $4\frac{3}{5}$ 11) $5\frac{3}{4}$ 16) $2\frac{5}{6}$

2) $11\frac{3}{10}$ 7) $3\frac{5}{7}$ 12) $8\frac{17}{35}$ 17) $4\frac{3}{4}$

3) $10\frac{7}{10}$ 8) $3\frac{2}{3}$ 13) $4\frac{2}{3}$ 18) $7\frac{5}{6}$

4) $9\frac{5}{6}$ 9) $4\frac{9}{25}$ 14) $5\frac{17}{35}$

5) $2\frac{2}{3}$ 10) $8\frac{3}{4}$ 15) $4\frac{7}{10}$

Chapter 5: Decimals

Topics that you'll learn in this chapter:

- ✓ Adding and Subtracting Decimals

- ✓ Multiplying and Dividing Decimals

- ✓ Order and Comparing Decimals

- ✓ Round decimals

- ✓ Comparing Decimals

Adding and Subtracting Decimals

✏️ Add and subtract decimals.

1)
$$\begin{array}{r} 18.14 \\ -\ 11.18 \\ \hline \end{array}$$

4)
$$\begin{array}{r} 46.18 \\ -\ 23.45 \\ \hline \end{array}$$

2)
$$\begin{array}{r} 39.72 \\ +\ 23.67 \\ \hline \end{array}$$

5)
$$\begin{array}{r} 80.30 \\ +\ 27.97 \\ \hline \end{array}$$

3)
$$\begin{array}{r} 83.36 \\ +\ 12.18 \\ \hline \end{array}$$

6)
$$\begin{array}{r} 66.68 \\ -\ 21.39 \\ \hline \end{array}$$

✏️ Solve.

7) _____ $+ 1.3 = 6.7$

10) $3.7 +$ _____ $= 14.4$

8) $4.2 +$ _____ $= 10.6$

11) _____ $+ 5.1 = 10.7$

9) $8.9 +$ _____ $= 18$

12) _____ $+ 9.9 = 15.2$

✏️ Order each set of numbers from least to greatest.

1) 0.3, 0.63, 0.33, 0.88, 0.46 ___, ___, ___, ___, ___, ___

2) 4.2, 5.4, 4.35, 6.86, 4.80 ___, ___, ___, ___, ___, ___

3) 1.2, 1.1, 0.8, 0.56, 0.23 ___, ___, ___, ___, ___, ___

4) 1.6, 4.4, 1.2, 4.2, 1.74, 3.45 ___, ___, ___, ___, ___, ___

5) 4.6, 7.2, 4.5, 6.7, 3.3, 3.43 ___, ___, ___, ___, ___, ___

6) 0.78, 0.98, 0.23, 1.06, 2.2 ___, ___, ___, ___, ___, ___

Multiplying and Dividing Decimals

✍ Find each product.

1) $\begin{array}{r} 2.4 \\ \times\ 1.3 \\ \hline \end{array}$

2) $\begin{array}{r} 6.7 \\ \times\ 4.8 \\ \hline \end{array}$

3) $\begin{array}{r} 1.5 \\ \times\ 1.3 \\ \hline \end{array}$

4) $\begin{array}{r} 3.9 \\ \times\ 5.7 \\ \hline \end{array}$

5) $\begin{array}{r} 11.1 \\ \times\ 9.6 \\ \hline \end{array}$

6) $\begin{array}{r} 2.5 \\ \times\ 5.3 \\ \hline \end{array}$

7) $\begin{array}{r} 3.7 \\ \times\ 7.3 \\ \hline \end{array}$

8) $\begin{array}{r} 98.20 \\ \times\ 100 \\ \hline \end{array}$

9) $\begin{array}{r} 10.12 \\ \times\ 5.9 \\ \hline \end{array}$

✍ Find each quotient.

10) $2.5 \div 0.98$

11) $18.4 \div 2.8$

12) $27.82 \div 6.7$

13) $8.5 \div 5.2$

14) $1.9 \div 10$

15) $9.2 \div 100$

16) $6.24 \div 10$

17) $8.5 \div 100$

18) $7.14 \div 1.34$

19) $16.24 \div 100$

Rounding Decimals

✏️ Round each decimal number to the nearest place indicated.

1) 0.2_4_

2) 4.0_3_

3) 6.6_12_

4) 0.2_89_

5) 6_.34

6) 0.2_9_

7) 9.2_1_

8) 7_.1260

9) 4.42_9_

10) 6.3_912

11) 3_.8

12) 3_.3529

13) 7.8_87

14) 2.5_3_

15) 50_.96

16) 65_.84

17) 35.7_9_

18) 835_.885

19) 46_.3

20) 35_.81

21) 7_.308

22) 96_.2

23) 216.5_32

24) 6.0_9_

Comparing Decimals

✍ Write the correct comparison symbol (>, < or =).

1) 0.26 ___ 2.4

2) 1.5 ___ 1.25

3) 7.1 ___ 7.1

4) 3.43 ___ 34.3

5) 4.65 ___ 0.465

6) 8.2 ___ 8

7) 8.1 ___ 0.81

8) 7.23 ___ 0.723

9) 6 ___ 0.6

10) 5.35 ___ 0.535

11) 13.3 ___ 13.5

12) 3.66 ___ 3.67

13) 6.08 ___ 6.22

14) 6.11 ___ 0.611

15) 7.89 ___ 7.86

16) 1.52 ___ 1.57

17) 3.52 ___ 0.352

18) 0.54 ___ 0.054

19) 19.4 ___ 19.4

20) 0.05 ___ 0.50

21) 0.69 ___ 0.7

22) 0.4 ___ 0.04

23) 0.30 ___ 0.3

24) 1.29 ___ 12.9

Answers of Worksheets – Chapter 5

Adding and Subtracting Decimals

1) 6.96	4) 22.73	7) 5.4	10) 10.7
2) 63.39	5) 108.27	8) 6.4	11) 5.6
3) 95.54	6) 45.29	9) 9.1	12) 5.3

Order and Comparing Decimals

1) 0.3, 0.33, 0.46, 0.63, 0.88   4) 1.2, 1.4, 1.6, 1.74, 4.2, 3.45

2) 4.2, 4.35, 4.80, 5.4, 6.86   5) 3.3, 3.43, 4.5, 4.6, 6.7, 7.2

3) 0.23, 0.56, 0.8, 1.1, 1.2   6) 0.23, 0.78, 0.98, 1.06, 2.2

Multiplying and Dividing Decimals

1) 3.12	6) 13.25	11) 6.571...	16) 0.624
2) 32.16	7) 27.01	12) 4.152...	17) 0.085
3) 1.95	8) 9,820	13) 1.634...	18) 5.328
4) 22.23	9) 59.708	14) 0.19	19) 0.1624
5) 106.56	10) 2.551...	15) 0.092	

Rounding Decimals

1) 0.2	7) 9.2	13) 7.9	19) 46
2) 4.0	8) 7	14) 2.5	20) 36
3) 6.6	9) 4.43	15) 51	21) 7
4) 0.3	10) 6.4	16) 66	22) 96
5) 6	11) 4	17) 35.8	23) 216.5
6) 0.3	12) 3	18) 836	24) 6.1

Comparing Decimals

1) 0.26 < 2.4	9) 6 > 0.6	17) 3.52 > 0.352
2) 1.5 > 1.25	10) 5.35 > 0.535	18) 0.54 > 0.054
3) 7.1 = 7.1	11) 13.3 < 13.5	19) 19.4 = 19.4
4) 3.43 < 34.3	12) 3.66 < 3.67	20) 0.05 < 0.50
5) 4.65 > 0.465	13) 6.08 < 6.22	21) 0.69 < 0.7
6) 8.2 > 8	14) 6.11 > 0.611	22) 0.4 > 0.04
7) 8.1 > 0.81	15) 7.89 > 7.86	23) 0.30 = 0.3
8) 7.23 > 0.73	16) 1.52 < 1.57	24) 1.29 < 12.9

Chapter 6: Ratios and rates

Topics that you'll learn in this chapter:

✓ Simplifying Ratios

✓ Writing Ratios

✓ Create a Proportion

✓ Proportional Ratios

✓ Ratio and Rates Word Problems

✓ Similar Figures

✓ Similar Figure Word Problems (Scale drawings: word problems)

Simplifying Ratios

✍Reduce each ratio.

1) 16: 64	9) 20: 16	17) 4: 44
2) 10: 30	10) 9: 18	18) 5: 20
3) 7: 14	11) 40: 56	19) 2: 50
4) 21: 18	12) 4: 36	20) 3: 30
5) 30: 35	13) 10: 15	21) 9: 27
6) 18: 14	14) 12: 30	22) 16: 72
7) 400: 20	15) 48: 8	23) 51: 60
8) 9: 6	16) 20: 40	24) 10: 100

Writing Ratios

✍Express each ratio as a rate and unite rate.

1) 150 miles on 5 gallons of gas.

2) 81 dollars for 9 books.

3) 300 miles on 30 gallons of gas

4) 45 inches of snow in 9 hours

✍Express each ratio as a fraction in the simplest form.

5) 5 feet out of 50 feet	11) 21 miles out of 72 miles
6) 10 cakes out of 35 cakes	12) 8 blue cars out of 20 cars
7) 24 dimes t0 45 dimes	13) 10 pennies to 100 pennies
8) 16 dimes out of 56 coins	14) 12 beetles out of 60 insects
9) 11 cups to 77 cups	15) 13 dimes to 39 dimes
10) 24 gallons to 36 gallons	16) 25 red cars out of 100 cars

Create a Proportion

✍ Create proportion from the given set of numbers.

1) 1, 12, 3, 4

2) 10, 110, 1, 11

3) 3, 9, 7, 21

4) 2, 5, 8, 20

5) 7, 2, 28, 8

6) 2, 3, 1, 6

7) 15, 5, 12, 4

8) 7, 2, 35, 10

9) 3, 24, 16, 2

10) 9, 27, 1, 3

11) 4, 1, 5, 20

12) 9, 16, 27, 48

Proportional Ratios

✍ Solve each proportion.

1) $\frac{3}{6} = \frac{2}{d}$

2) $\frac{k}{5} = \frac{4}{10}$

3) $\frac{20}{5} = \frac{6}{x}$

4) $\frac{x}{3} = \frac{1}{6}$

5) $\frac{d}{3} = \frac{3}{9}$

6) $\frac{15}{7} = \frac{30}{x}$

7) $\frac{8}{10} = \frac{k}{30}$

8) $\frac{100}{25} = \frac{10}{d}$

9) $\frac{x}{14} = \frac{6}{21}$

10) $\frac{15}{3} = \frac{x}{2}$

11) $\frac{12}{x} = \frac{12}{4}$

12) $\frac{x}{4} = \frac{36}{18}$

13) $\frac{40}{10} = \frac{k}{20}$

14) $\frac{36}{6} = \frac{18}{d}$

15) $\frac{x}{8} = \frac{20}{10}$

16) $\frac{9}{7} = \frac{k}{7}$

17) $\frac{20}{15} = \frac{15}{d}$

18) $\frac{40}{x} = \frac{20}{3}$

19) $\frac{d}{6} = \frac{18}{12}$

20) $\frac{k}{8} = \frac{8}{4}$

21) $\frac{12}{6} = \frac{x}{7}$

22) $\frac{30}{10} = \frac{k}{20}$

23) $\frac{13}{26} = \frac{x}{4}$

24) $\frac{8}{22} = \frac{x}{11}$

Similar Figures

✍ Each pair of figures is similar. Find the missing side.

1)

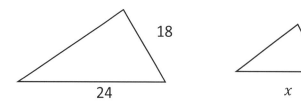

2)

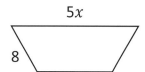 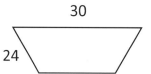

3)

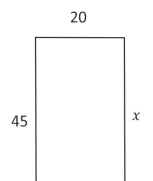 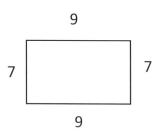

Word Problems

⚓ Solve.

1) In a party, 10 soft drinks are required for every 24 guests. If there are 480 guests, how many soft drinks is required?

2) In Jack's class, 24 of the students are tall and 15 are short. In Michael's class 56 students are tall and 35 students are short. Which class has a higher ratio of tall to short students?

3) Are these ratios equivalent?

10 cards to 70 animals 13 marbles to 91 marbles

4) The price of 5 apples at the Quick Market is $2.45. The price of 8 of the same apples at Walmart is $4.16. Which place is the better buy?

5) The bakers at a Bakery can make 200 bagels in 5 hours. How many bagels can they bake in 12 hours? What is that rate per hour?

⚠Answer each question and round your answer to the nearest whole number.

6) If a 48.9 ft tall flagpole casts a 280.98 ft long shadow, then how long is the shadow that a 6.3 ft tall woman casts?

7) A model igloo has a scale of 1 in: 4 ft. If the real igloo is 24 ft wide, then how wide is the model igloo?

8) If a 45 ft tall tree casts a 9 ft long shadow, then how tall is an adult giraffe that casts a 6 ft shadow?

9) Find the distance between San Joe and Mount Pleasant if they are 3 cm apart on a map with a scale of 1 cm: 4 km.

10) A telephone booth that is 14 ft tall casts a shadow that is 7 ft long. Find the height of a lawn ornament that casts a 3 ft shadow.

Answers of Worksheets – Chapter 6

Simplifying Ratios

1) 2: 8	7) 20: 1	13) 2: 3	19) 1: 25
2) 1: 3	8) 3: 2	14) 2: 5	20) 1: 10
3) 1: 7	9) 5: 4	15) 6: 1	21) 1: 3
4) 7: 6	10) 1: 2	16) 1: 2	22) 2: 9
5) 6: 7	11) 5: 7	17) 1: 11	23) 17: 20
6) 9: 7	12) 1: 9	18) 1: 4	24) 1: 10

Writing Ratios

1) $\frac{150 \text{ miles}}{5 \text{ gallons}}$, 30 miles per gallon

3) $\frac{300 \text{ miles}}{30 \text{ gallons}}$, 10 miles per gallon

2) $\frac{81 \text{ dollars}}{9 \text{ books}}$, 9.00 dollars per book

4) $\frac{45" \text{ of snow}}{9 \text{ hours}}$, 5 inches of snow per hour

5) $\frac{1}{10}$	8) $\frac{2}{7}$	11) $\frac{7}{24}$	14) $\frac{1}{5}$
6) $\frac{2}{7}$	9) $\frac{1}{7}$	12) $\frac{2}{5}$	15) $\frac{1}{3}$
7) $\frac{8}{15}$	10) $\frac{2}{3}$	13) $\frac{1}{10}$	16) $\frac{1}{4}$

Create Proportion

1) 1: 4 = 3: 12	5) 7: 2 =28: 8	9) 2: 3 = 16: 24
2) 10: 110 = 1: 11	6) 6: 3 = 2: 1	10) 27: 9 = 3: 1
3) 7: 3 = 21: 9	7) 12: 15 = 4: 5	11) 4: 1 = 20: 5
4) 5: 2 = 15: 6	8) 7: 2 = 35: 10	12) 27: 9 = 48: 16

Proportional Ratios

1) 4	7) 24	13) 80	19) 9
2) 2	8) 2.5	14) 3	20) 16
3) 1.5	9) 4	15) 16	21) 14
4) 0.5	10) 10	16) 9	22) 60
5) 1	11) 4	17) 11.25	23) 2
6) 14	12) 8	18) 6	24) 4

Similar Figures

1) 4	2) 2	3) 45

Word Problems

1) 200

2) The ratio for both classes is equal to 8 to 5.

3) Yes! Both ratios are 1 to 7

4) The price at the Quick Market is a better buy.

5) 480, the rate is 40 per hour.

6) 36.2 ft

7) 6 in

8) 30 ft

9) 12 km

10) 6 ft

Chapter 7: Algebra

Topics that you'll learn in this chapter:

- ✓ Find a Rule between input and output

- ✓ Variables and Expressions

- ✓ Evaluating Variable

- ✓ Evaluating Two Variables

- ✓ Solve Equations

Find a Rule

✍ Complete the output.

1- **Rule:** the output is $x - 15$

Input	x	19	28	42	45	56
Output	y					

2- **Rule:** the output is $x \times 28$

Input	x	2	4	6	8	30
Output	y					

3- **Rule:** the output is $x \div 7$

Input	x	469	245	280	196	147
Output	y					

✍ Find a rule to write an expression.

4- **Rule:** _____

Input	x	8	16	20	28
Output	y	24	48	60	84

5- **Rule:** _____

Input	x	8	21	35	49
Output	y	16	29	43	57

6- **Rule:** _____

Input	x	99	162	261	288
Output	y	11	18	29	32

Variables and Expressions

✎Write a verbal expression for each algebraic expression.

1) $2a - 4b$

2) $6c^2 + 2d$

3) $x - 17$

4) $\dfrac{80}{5}$

5) $a^2 + b^3$

6) $2x + 4$

7) $x^2 - 10y + 18$

8) $x^3 + 9y^2 - 4$

9) $\dfrac{1}{3}x + \dfrac{3}{4}y - 6$

10) $\dfrac{1}{5}(x + 8) - 10y$

✎Write an algebraic expression for each verbal expression.

11) 9 less than h

12) The product of 10 and b

13) The 20 divided by K

14) The product of 5 and the third power of x

15) 10 more than h to the fifth power

16) 20 more than twice d

17) One fourth the square of b

18) The difference of 23 and 4 times a number

19) 60 more than the cube of a number

20) Three-quarters the cube of a number

Evaluating Variable

✍ Simplify each algebraic expression.

1) $12 - x$, $x = 4$

2) $x + 10$, $x = 1$

3) $5x + 7$, $x = -2$

4) $2x + (-7)$, $x = -3$

5) $3x - 16$, $x = 2$

6) $5x + 6$, $x = -2$

7) $10 + 9x - 16$, $x = 2$

8) $11 - 2x$, $x = 7$

9) $\frac{40}{x} - 3$, $x = 5$

10) $(-13) + \frac{x}{2} + 2x, x = 8$

11) $(-8) + \frac{x}{6}, x = 42$

12) $\left(-\frac{20}{x}\right) - 8 + 9x$, $x = 2$

13) $\left(-\frac{27}{x}\right) - 9 + 5x$, $x = 3$

14) $(-4) + \frac{x}{5}$, $x = 25$

15) $5(15x + 10)$, $x = -1$

16) $12x + 14x - 20 + 2$,

$x = 1$

17) $\left(-\frac{12}{x}\right) + 12 + 3x$,

$x = 3$

18) $4(-3a + 6a)$,

$a = 4$

19) $15 - 6x + 17 - 2x$,

$x = 5$

20) $19x - 16 - 4x$,

$x = 3$

21) $20 - 3(3x + x)$, $x = 1$

Solve Equations

✍ Solve each equation.

1) $2x + 5 = 15$

2) $25 = (-5) + 2x$

3) $6x = 66$

4) $64 = 4x$

5) $(-6) = 16 + 2x$

6) $7 + 2x = (-3)$

7) $20x = 140$

8) $20 = 2x + 4$

9) $(-36) + x = (-20)$

10) $9x = 63$

11) $2x - 12 = (-46)$

12) $x - 13 = (-25)$

13) $(-60) = x - 45$

14) $24 = 3x$

15) $2x = 34$

16) $99 = 9x$

17) $x - 140 = 20$

18) $9x = 81$

19) $32 = 8x$

20) $2x = 72$

21) $2x + 28 = 40$

22) $2x - 15 = 31$

23) $45 + 2x - 21 = 0$

24) $90x = 900$

Answers of Worksheets – Chapter 7

Find a Rule

1)

Input	x	19	28	42	45	56
Output	y	4	13	27	30	41

2)

Input	x	2	4	6	8	30
Output	y	56	112	168	224	840

3)

Input	x	469	245	280	196	147
Output	y	67	35	40	28	21

4) y = 3x   5) y = x + 8   6) y = x ÷ 9

Variables and Expressions

1) 2 times a minus 4 times b

2) 6 times c squared plus 2 times d

3) a number minus 17

4) the quotient of 80 and 5

5) a squared plus b cubed

6) the product of 2 and x plus 4

7) x squared plus the product of 10 and y plus 18

8) x cubed plus the product of 9 and y squared minus the product of 4 and y

9) the sum of one–thirds of x and three–quarters of y, minus 6

10) one–sixth of the sum of x and 8 minus the product of 10 and y

11) 9<h

12) 10b

13) $\frac{20}{K}$

14) $5x^3$

15) $10 > h^5$

16) $2d < 20$

17) $\frac{1}{4}b^2$

18) $23 - 4a$

19) $60 > a^3$

20) $\frac{3}{4}x^3$

Evaluating Variable

1) 8

2) 11

3) −3

4) −13

5) −10

6) −4

7) 12

8) −3

9) 5

10) 7

11) −1

12) 0

13) −3

14) 1

15) −25

16) 8

17) 17

18) 48

19) −8

20) 29

21) 8

Solve Equations

1) 5

2) 15

3) 11

4) 16

5) − 11

6) − 5

7) 7

8) 8

9) 16

10) 7

11) − 17

12) − 12

13) − 15

14) 8

15) 17

16) 11

17) 160

18) 9

19) 4

20) 36

21) 6

22) 23

23) −12

24) 10

Chapter 8: Measurement

Topics that you'll learn in this chapter:

- ✓ Reference Measurement
- ✓ Metric Length
- ✓ Customary Length
- ✓ Metric Capacity
- ✓ Customary Capacity
- ✓ Metric Weight and Mass
- ✓ Customary Weight and Mass
- ✓ Time
- ✓ Add Money Amounts
- ✓ Subtract Money Amounts
- ✓ Money: Word Problems

Reference Measurement

LENGTH

Customary	Metric
1 mile (mi) = 1,760 yards (yd)	1 kilometer (km) = 1,000 meters (m)
1 yard (yd) = 3 feet (ft)	1 meter (m) = 100 centimeters (cm)
1 foot (ft) = 12 inches (in.)	1 centimeter(cm)= 10 millimeters(mm)

VOLUME AND CAPACITY

Customary	Metric
1 gallon (gal) = 4 quarts (qt)	1 liter (L) = 1,000 milliliters (mL)
1 quart (qt) = 2 pints (pt.)	
1 pint (pt.) = 2 cups (c)	
1 cup (c) = 8 fluid ounces (Fl oz)	

WEIGHT AND MASS

Customary	Metric
1 ton (T) = 2,000 pounds (lb.)	1 kilogram (kg) = 1,000 grams (g)
1 pound (lb.) = 16 ounces (oz)	1 gram (g) = 1,000 milligrams (mg)

Time

1 year = 12 months

1 year = 52 weeks

1 week = 7 days

1 day = 24 hours

1 hour = 60 minutes

1 minute = 60 seconds

Metric Length Measurement

✍Convert to the units.

1) 200 mm = _____ cm

2) 4 m = _____ mm

3) 5 m = _____ cm

4) 6 km = _____ m

5) 8,000mm = _____ m

6) 900 cm = _____ m

7) 11 m = _____ cm

8) 2,000 mm = _____ cm

9) 4,000 mm = _____ m

10) 6 km = _____ mm

11) 12 km = _____ m

12) 40 m = _____ cm

13) 8,000 m = _____ km

14) 9,000 m = _____ km

Customary Length Measurement

✍Convert to the units.

1) 6 ft = _____ in

2) 3 ft = _____ in

3) 3 yd = _____ ft

4) 5 yd = _____ ft

5) 3 yd = _____ in

6) 36 in = _____ ft

7) 252 in = ____ yd

8) 180in = _____ yd

9) 20yd = _____ in

10) 58yd = _____ in

11) 81ft = _____ yd

12) 150ft = _____ yd

13) 96in = _____ ft

14) 60 yd = _____ feet

Metric Capacity Measurement

✍ Convert the following measurements.

1) 40 l = _____ ml

2) 6 l = _____ ml

3) 40 l = _____ ml

4) 32 l = _____ ml

5) 27 l = _____ ml

6) 13 l = _____ ml

7) 80,000 l = _____ l

8) 56,000mml = _____ l

9) 95,000ml = _____ l

10) 4,000 ml = _____ l

11) 10,000 ml = _____ l

12) 70, 000 ml = _____ l

Customary Capacity Measurement

✍ Convert the following measurements.

1) 78gal = _____ qt.

2) 44gal = _____ pt.

3) 75gal = _____ c.

4) 15pt. = _____ c

5) 18 qt = _____ pt.

6) 19qt= _____ c

7) 28pt. = _____ c

8) 64c = _____ gal

9) 128pt. = _____ gal

10) 112qt = _____ gal

11) 164pt. = _____ qt

12) 88c = _____ qt

13) 156c = _____ pt.

14) 192 qt= _____ gal

15) 130pt. = _____ qt

16) 86gal = _____ pt.

Metric Weight and Mass Measurement

✍Convert.

1) 40 kg = _____ g

2) 45 kg = _____ g

3) 500 kg = _____ g

4) 50 kg = _____ g

5) 55 kg = _____ g

6) 80 kg = _____ g

7) 78 kg = _____ g

8) 62,000 g = _____ kg

9) 530,000 g = _____ kg

10) 400,000 g = _____ kg

11) 30,000 g = _____ kg

12) 20,000 g = _____ kg

13) 850,000 g = _____ kg

14) 900,000 g = _____ kg

Customary Weight and Mass Measurement

✍Convert.

1) 6,000 lb. = _____ T

2) 12,000 lb. = _____ T

3) 8,000 lb. = _____ T

4) 14,000lb. = _____ T

5) 32 lb. = _____ oz

6) 46lb.= _____ oz

7) 135lb. = _____ oz

8) 2T = _____ lb.

9) 9T = _____ lb.

10) 12T = _____ lb.

11) 15T = _____ lb.

12) 8T = _____ oz

13) 6T = _____ oz

14) 13T= _____ oz

100.5

Temperature

– 17, 2 2 2 2 2 2

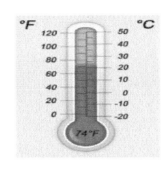

$(7\overline{F}-32)\times\dfrac{5}{9}$

$F = 38°$.

✎ Convert Fahrenheit into Celsius.

1) $14°F = \underline{\hspace{1cm}} °C$

2) $17.6°F = \underline{\hspace{1cm}} °C$

3) $23°F = \underline{\hspace{1cm}} °C$

4) $33.8°F = \underline{\hspace{1cm}} °C$

5) $68°F = \underline{\hspace{1cm}} °C$

6) $86°F = \underline{\hspace{1cm}} °C$

7) $98.6°F = \underline{\hspace{1cm}} °C$

8) $104°F = \underline{\hspace{1cm}} °C$

9) $44.6°F = \underline{\hspace{1cm}} °C$

10) $158°F = \underline{\hspace{1cm}} °C$

11) $176°F = \underline{\hspace{1cm}} °C$

12) $392°F = \underline{\hspace{1cm}} °C$

✎ Convert Celsius into Fahrenheit.

13) $0°C = \underline{\hspace{1cm}} °F$

14) $10°C = \underline{\hspace{1cm}} °F$

15) $20°C = \underline{\hspace{1cm}} °F$

16) $37°C = \underline{\hspace{1cm}} °F$

17) $50°C = \underline{\hspace{1cm}} °F$

18) $80°C = \underline{\hspace{1cm}} °F$

19) $90°C = \underline{\hspace{1cm}} °F$

20) $100°C = \underline{\hspace{1cm}} °F$

21) $2°C = \underline{\hspace{1cm}} °F$

22) $45°C = \underline{\hspace{1cm}} °F$

23) $68°C = \underline{\hspace{1cm}} °F$

24) $38°C = \underline{\hspace{1cm}} °F$

Time

✎ Convert to the units.

1) 20 hr. = _____ min

2) 14 year = _____ week

3) 7hr = _____ sec

4) 72min = _____ sec

5) 2,400min = _____ hr.

6) 1,095day = _____ year

7) 2year = _____ hr.

8) 35day = _____ hr.

9) 3 day = _____ min

10) 420min = _____ hr.

11) 20year = _____ month

12) 3,000sec = _____ min

13) 216hr = _____ day

14) 15 weeks = _____ day

✎ How much time has passed?

1) From 1:15 A.M. to 4:25 A.M.: ____ hours and ___ minutes.

2) From 2:20 A.M. to 6:45 A.M.: ____ hours and ___ minutes.

3) It's 8:40 P.M. What time was 4 hours ago? _____ O'clock

4) 3:20 A.M to 6:40 AM: _____ hours and _____ minutes.

5) 2:35 A.M to 6:55 AM: _____ hours and _____ minutes.

6) 8:00 A.M. to 10:25 AM. = _____ hour(s) and _____ minutes.

7) 9:45 A.M. to 2:15 PM. = _____ hour(s) and _____ minutes

8) 9:15 A.M. to 9:50 A.M. = _____ minutes

9) 4:05 A.M. to 4:52 A.M. = _____ minutes

Money Amounts

✎ Add.

1)
$104
+$232
_____

$402
+$310
_____

$220
+$115
_____

2)
$521
+$330
_____

$330
+$401
_____

$532
+$342
_____

3)
$421
+$202
_____

$510
+$228
_____

$640
+$210
_____

4)
$521.50
+$123.70
_____

$611.20
+$320.75
_____

$415.00
+$256.30
_____

✎ Subtract.

5)
$535
−$123
_____

$441
−$130
_____

$745
−$424
_____

6)
$526
−$127
_____

$489
−$316
_____

$540
−$439
_____

7)
$446.30
−$119.50
_____

$746.50
−$228.80
_____

$742.70
−$389.50
_____

8) Linda had $13.50. She bought some game tickets for $7.15. How much did she have left?

Money: Word Problems

✎Solve.

1) How many boxes of envelopes can you buy with $30 if one box costs $5?

2) After paying $5.12 for a salad, Ella has $41.46. How much money did she have before buying the salad?

3) How many packages of diapers can you buy with $84 if one package costs $4?

4) Last week James ran 35 miles more than Michael. James ran 68 miles. How many miles did Michael run?

5) Last Friday Jacob had $26.52. Over the weekend he received some money for cleaning the attic. He now has $45. How much money did he receive?

6) After paying $4.08 for a sandwich, Amelia has $37.50. How much money did she have before buying the sandwich?

Answers of Worksheets – Chapter 8

Metric length

1) 20 cm

2) 4,000 mm

3) 500 cm

4) 6,000 m

5) 8 m

6) 9 m

7) 1,100 cm

8) 20 cm

9) 4 m

10) 6,000,000 mm

11) 12,000 m

12) 4,000 cm

13) 8 km

14) 9 km

Customary Length

1) 72

2) 36

3) 9

4) 15

5) 108

6) 3

7) 7

8) 5

9) 720

10) 2,088

11) 27

12) 50

13) 8

14) 180

Metric Capacity

1) 40,000 ml

2) 6,000 ml

3) 40,000 ml

4) 32,000 ml

5) 27,000 ml

6) 13,000 ml

7) 80 ml

8) 56 ml

9) 95 ml

10) 4L

11) 10 L

12) 70 L

Customary Capacity

1) 312 qt

2) 352 pt.

3) 1,200 c

4) 30 c

5) 36 pt.

6) 76c

7) 56 c

8) 8 gal

9) 16 gal

10) 28 gal

11) 82 qt

12) 22qt

13) 78 pt.

14) 48 gal

15) 65 qt

16) 688 pt.

Metric Weight and Mass

1) 40,000 g

2) 45,000 g

3) 500,000 g

4) 50,000 g

5) 55,000 g

6) 80,000 g

7) 78,000 g

8) 62 kg

9) 530 kg

10) 400 kg

11) 30 kg

12) 20 kg

13) 850 kg

14) 900 kg

Customary Weight and Mass

1) 3 T	6) 736 oz	11) 30,000 lb.
2) 6 T	7) 2,160 oz	12) 256,000 oz
3) 4 T	8) 4,000 lb.	13) 192,000 oz
4) 7 T	9) 18,000 lb.	14) 416,000 oz
5) 512 oz	10) 24,000 lb.	

Temperature

1) −10°C	7) 37°C	13) 32°F	19) 194°F
2) −8°C	8) 40°C	14) 50°F	20) 212°F
3) −5°C	9) 7°C	15) 68°F	21) 35.6°F
4) 1°C	10) 70°C	16) 98.6°F	22) 113°F
5) 20°C	11) 80°C	17) 122°F	23) 154.4°F
6) 30°C	12) 200°C	18) 176°F	24) 100.4°F

Time - Convert

1) 1,200 min	6) 3 year	11) 240 months
2) 728 weeks	7) 17,520hr	12) 50 min
3) 2,520 sec	8) 840 hr	13) 9 days
4) 4,320 sec	9) 4,320 min	14) 105 days
5) 40 hr	10) 7hr	

Time - Gap

1) 3:10	4) 3:20	7) 4:30
2) 4:25	5) 4:20	8) 35 minutes
3) 4:40P.M.	6) 2:25	9) 47 minutes

Add Money

1) 336, 712, 335	3) 623, 738, 850
2) 851, 731, 874	4) 645.2,931.95, 671.30

Subtract Money

5) 412–311–321	7) 326.80–517.70–353.20
6) 399–173–101	8) $6.35

Money: word problem

1) 6	3) 21	5) 18.48
2) $46.58	4) 33	6) 41.58

Chapter 9: Geometric

Topics that you'll learn in this chapter:

- ✓ Identifying Angles: Acute, Right, Obtuse, and Straight Angles

- ✓ Estimate and Measure Angles with a Protractor

- ✓ Polygon Names

- ✓ Classify Triangles

- ✓ Parallel Sides in Quadrilaterals

- ✓ Identify Parallelograms

- ✓ Identify Trapezoids

- ✓ Identify Rectangles

- ✓ Perimeter and Area of Squares

- ✓ Perimeter and Area of rectangles

- ✓ Area and Perimeter: Word Problems

- ✓ Circumference, Diameter and Radius

- ✓ Volume of Cubes and Rectangle Prisms

Identifying Angles

✍ Write the name of the angles (Acute, Right, Obtuse, and Straight).

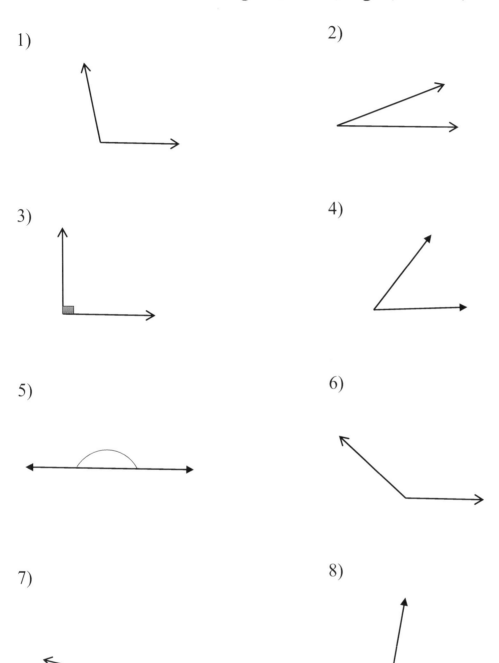

1)

2)

3)

4)

5)

6)

7)

8)

Estimate Angle Measurements

✍ Estimate the approximate measurement of each angle in degrees.

1)

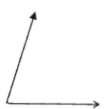

2)

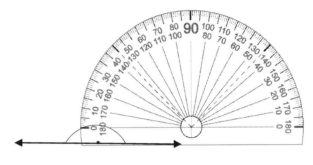

3)

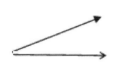

4)

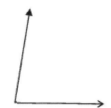

5)

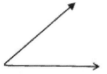

6)

7)

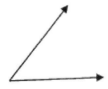

8)

Measure Angles with a Protractor

✍ Use protractor to measure the angles below.

1)

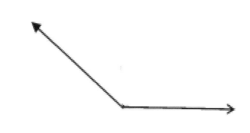

2)

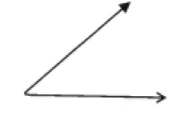

3)

4)

✍ Use a protractor to draw angles for each measurement given.

1) 30◦

2) 95◦

3) 150◦

4) 60

5) 45

Polygon Names

✍ Write name of polygons.

1)

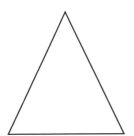

2)

3)

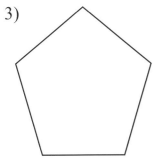

4)

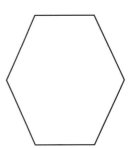

5)

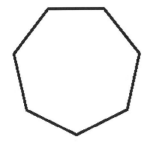

6)

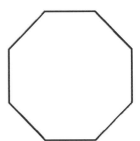

Classify Triangles

✍ Classify the triangles by their sides and angles.

1)

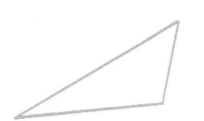

2)

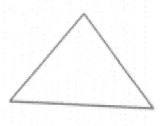

3)

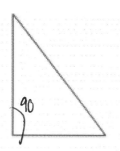

4)

5)

6)

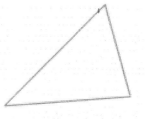

Parallel Sides in Quadrilaterals

✎ Write name of quadrilaterals.

1) Squar

2)

3)

4)

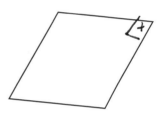

5)

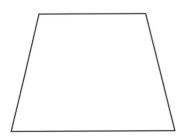

6)

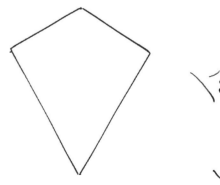

Identify Rectangles

✎ Solve.

1) A rectangle has _____ sides and _____ angles.

2) Draw a rectangle that is 7centimeters long and 3 centimeters wide. What is the perimeter?

3) Draw a rectangle 4 cm long and 2 cm wide.

4) Draw a rectangle whose length is 5 cm and whose width is 3 cm. What is the perimeter of the rectangle?

5) What is the perimeter of the rectangle?

6

8

Perimeter: Find the Missing Side Lengths

✎ Find the missing side of each shape.

1) perimeter = 80

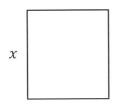

2) perimeter = 28

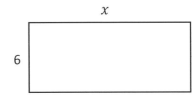

3) perimeter = 60

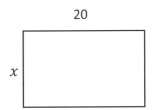

4) perimeter = 20

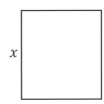

5) perimeter = 60

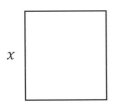

6) perimeter = 26

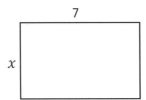

7) perimeter = 52

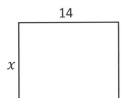

8) perimeter = 24

Perimeter and Area of Squares

Find perimeter and area of squares.

1) A: _____, P: _____

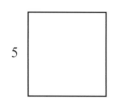
5

2) A: _____, P: _____

7

3) A: _____, P: _____

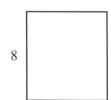
8

4) A: _____, P: _____

9

5) A: _____, P: _____

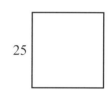
25

6) A: _____, P: _____

13

7) A: _____, P: _____

14

8) A: _____, P: _____

15

Perimeter and Area of rectangles

 Find perimeter and area of rectangles.

1) A: _____, P: _____

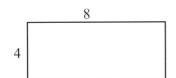

2) A: _____, P: _____

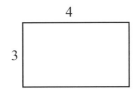

3) A: _____, P: _____

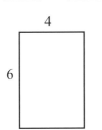

4) A: _____, P: _____

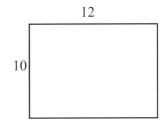

5) A: _____, P: _____

6) A: _____, P: _____

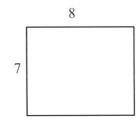

7) A: _____, P: _____

8) A: _____, P: _____

Find the Area or Missing Side Length of a Rectangle

 Find area or missing side length of rectangles.

1) Area =?

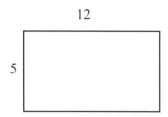

2) Area = 42, x=?

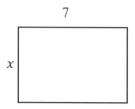

3) Area = 54, x=?

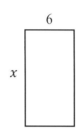

4) Area =?

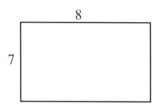

5) Area =?

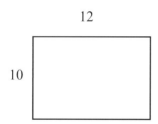

6) Area = 500, x=?

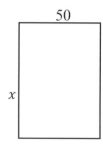

7) Area = 650, x=?

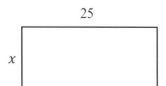

8) Area 624, x=?

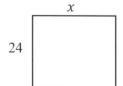

Area and Perimeter: Word Problems

✐Solve.

1) The area of a rectangle is 96 square meters. The width is 8 meters. What is the length of the rectangle?

2) A square has an area of 64 square feet. What is the perimeter of the square?

3) Ava built a rectangular vegetable garden that is 5 feet long and has an area of 45 square feet. What is the perimeter of Ava's vegetable garden?

4) A square has a perimeter of 96 millimeters. What is the area of the square?

5) The perimeter of David's square backyard is 88 meters. What is the area of David's backyard?

6) The area of a rectangle is 32 square inches. The length is 8 inches. What is the perimeter of the rectangle?

Circumference, Diameter, and Radius

✎ Find the diameter and circumference of circles.

1)

2)

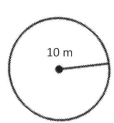

3)

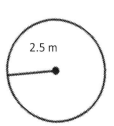

4)

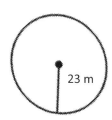

✎ Find the radius.

5)

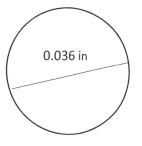

6)

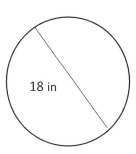

7) Diameter = 15*ft*

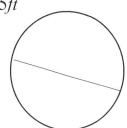

8) Diameter = 45 m

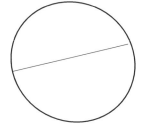

Volume of Cubes and Rectangle Prisms

✐Find the volume of each of the rectangular prisms.

1)

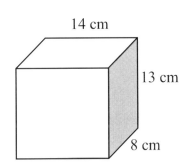

2)

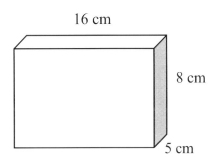

3)

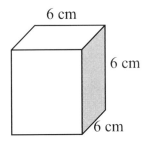

4)

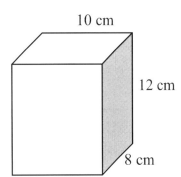

5)

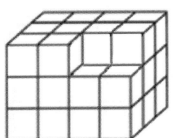

6)

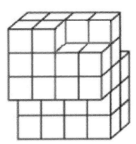

Answers of Worksheets – Chapter 9

Identifying Angles

1) Obtuse   3) Right   5) Straight   7) Obtuse

2) Acute   4) Acute   6) Obtuse   8) Acute

Estimate Angle Measurements

1) 70°   3) 20°   5) 40°   7) 50°

2) 180°   4) 80°   6) 135°   8) 100°

Measure Angles with a Protractor

1) 140∘   2) 40∘   3) 135∘   4) 160∘

Draw angles

1)   2)   3)

   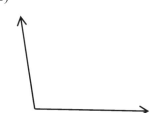   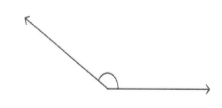

4)   5)

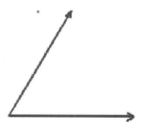   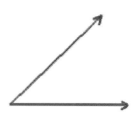

Polygon Names

1) Triangle   3) Pentagon   5) Heptagon

2) Quadrilateral   4) Hexagon   6) Octagon

Classify triangles

1) Scalene, obtuse   4) Equilateral, acute

2) Isosceles, right   5) Isosceles, acute

3) Scalene, right   6) Scalene, acute

Parallel Sides in Quadrilaterals

1) Square

2) Rectangle

3) Parallelogram

4) Rhombus

5) Trapezoid

6) Kike

Identify Rectangles

1) 4 - 4

2) 20

3) Draw the square

4) 16

5) 28

Perimeter: Find the Missing Side Lengths

1) 20

2) 8

3) 10

4) 5

5) 15

6) 6

7) 12

8) 6

Perimeter and Area of Squares

1) A: 25, P: 20

2) A: 49, P: 28

3) A: 64, P: 32

4) A: 81, P: 36

5) A: 625 P: 100

6) A: 169, P: 52

7) A: 196, P: 56

8) A: 225, P: 60

Perimeter and Area of rectangles

1) A: 32, P: 24

2) A: 12, P: 14

3) A: 24, P: 20

4) A: 120, P: 44

5) A: 44, P: 30

6) A: 56, P: 30

7) A: 50.4, P: 33.2

8) A: 116.8, P: 45.2

Find the Area or Missing Side Length of a Rectangle

1) 60

2) 6

3) 9

4) 56

5) 120

6) 10

7) 26

8) 26

Area and Perimeter: Word Problems

1) 12

2) 32

3) 28

4) 576

5) 484

6) 24

Circumference, Diameter, and Radius

1) diameter: 7.5 circumferences: 7.5 π or 23.55

2) diameter: 20 circumferences: 20π or 62.80

3) diameter: 5 circumferences: 5π or 15.7

4) diameter: 46 circumferences: 46π or 144.44

5) radius: 0.018 in

6) radius: 9 in

7) radius: 7.5 *ft*

8) radius: 22.5 m

Volume of Cubes and Rectangle Prisms

1) 1,456 cm^3

2) 640 cm^3

3) 216 c m^3

4) 960 cm^3

5) 34

6) 42

Chapter 10: Three-Dimensional Figures

Topics that you'll learn in this chapter:

✓ Identify Three–Dimensional Figures

✓ Count Vertices, Edges, and Faces

✓ Identify Faces of Three–Dimensional Figures

Identify Three–Dimensional Figures

✍ Write the name of each shape.

1) *cube*

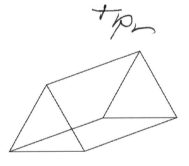

2) *TPir*

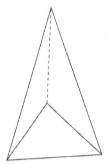

3) *TPr*

4)

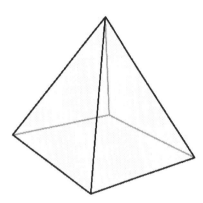

5)

6) *5*

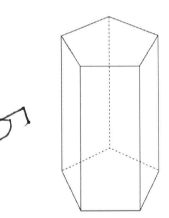

Count Vertices, Edges, and Faces

	Shape	Number of edges	Number of faces	Number of vertices
1)		6	4	4
2)		8	5	6
3)		12	6	8
4)		15	7	10
5)		18	8	12
6)		___	___	___

Identify Faces of Three–Dimensional Figures

✍ Write the number of faces.

1)

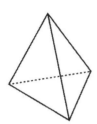

2)

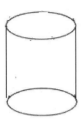

3)

4)

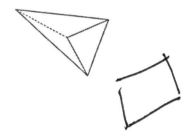

5)

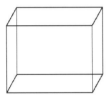

6)

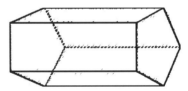

7)

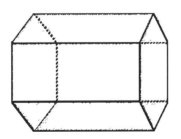

8)

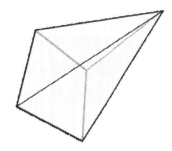

Answers of Worksheets – Chapter 10

Identify Three–Dimensional Figures

1) Cube

2) Triangular pyramid

3) Triangular prism

4) Square pyramid

5) Rectangular prism

6) Pentagonal prism

7) Hexagonal prism

Count Vertices, Edges, and Faces

Shape	Number of edges	Number of faces	Number of vertices
1)	6	4	4
2)	8	5	5
3)	12	6	8
4)	12	6	8
5)	15	7	10
6)	18	8	12

Identify Faces of Three–Dimensional Figures

1) 6

2) 2

3) 5

4) 4

5) 6

6) 7

7) 8

8) 5

Chapter 11: Symmetry and Transformations

Topics that you'll learn in this chapter:

- ✓ Line Segments

- ✓ Identify Lines of Symmetry

- ✓ Count Lines of Symmetry

- ✓ Parallel, Perpendicular and Intersecting Lines

- ✓ Translations, Rotations, and Reflections

Line Segments

✍ Write each as a line, ray or line segment.

1)

2)

3)

4)

5)

6)

7)

8)

Identify Lines of Symmetry

✍ Tell whether the line on each shape a line of symmetry is.

1)

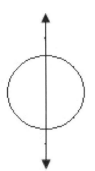

2)

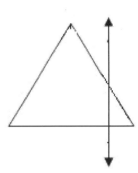

3)

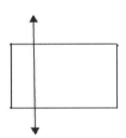

4)

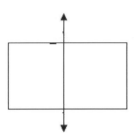

5)

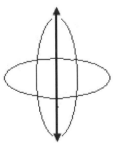

6)

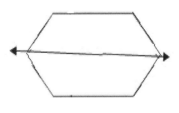

7)

8)

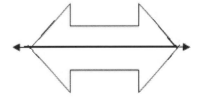

Count Lines of Symmetry

Draw lines of symmetry on each shape. Count and write the lines of symmetry you see.

1)

2)

3)

4)

5)

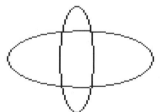

6)

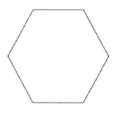

7)

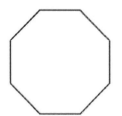

8)

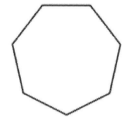

Parallel, Perpendicular and Intersecting Lines

✎ State whether the given pair of lines are parallel, perpendicular, or intersecting.

1)

2)

3)

4)

5)

6)

7)

8)

Answers of Worksheets – Chapter 11

Line Segments

1) Line segment

2) Ray

3) Line

4) Line segment

5) Ray

6) Line

7) Line

8) Line segment

Identify lines of symmetry

1) yes

2) no

3) no

4) yes

5) yes

6) yes

7) no

8) yes

Count lines of symmetry

1)

2)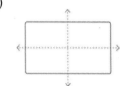

3)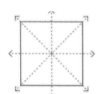

4)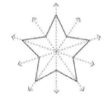

5)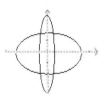

6)

7)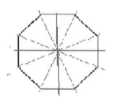

8)

Parallel, Perpendicular and Intersecting Lines

1) Perpendicular

2) Intersection

3) Parallel

4) Parallel

5) Parallel

6) Perpendicular

7) Intersection

8) Parallel

Chapter 12: Data and Graphs

Topics that you'll learn in this chapter:

- ✓ Graph Points on a Coordinate Plane

- ✓ Bar Graph

- ✓ Tally and Pictographs

- ✓ Line Graphs

- ✓ Stem–And–Leaf Plot

- ✓ Scatter Plots

Mean and Median

✎ Find Mean and Median of the Given Data.

1) $18, 16, 7, 1, 9$

2) $5, 16, 5, 17, 4, 13$

3) $13, 15, 11, 8, 19$

4) $5, 9, 1, 8, 6, 1$

5) $7, 6, 8, 5, 8, 11, 12$

6) $6, 1, 5, 5, 9, 14, 20$

7) $18, 4, 10, 5, 24, 6, 6, 21$

8) $28, 9, 2, 4, 19, 7, 22$

9) $38, 25, 41, 26, 33, 43, 61$

10) $11, 15, 1, 15, 4, 15, 8, 11$

11) $48, 16, 32, 64, 44, 33$

12) $37, 38, 58, 88, 43, 84$

13) $61, 69, 50, 57, 42, 44$

14) $96, 85, 82, 25, 71, 93, 39$

15) $98, 12, 101, 64, 37, 50$

16) $20, 77, 8, 99, 13, 46, 11$

✎ Solve.

17) In a javelin throw competition, five athletics score 76, 78, 68, 57 and 65 meters. What are their Mean and Median? _____

18) Eva went to shop and bought 13 apples, 4 peaches, 6 bananas, 2 pineapple and 5 melons. What are the Mean and Median of her purchase?

_____

Mode and Range

✍ Find Mode and Rage of the Given Data.

1) 10, 3, 5, 8, 7, 3

    Mode: _____ Range: _____

2) 7, 7, 12, 4, 17, 3, 9, 21

    Mode: _____ Range: _____

3) 2, 2, 1, 19, 8, 19, 2, 6, 2

    Mode: _____ Range: _____

4) 11, 29, 2, 29, 3, 6, 29, 7

    Mode: _____ Range: _____

5) 6, 6, 4, 6, 18, 4, 18

    Mode: _____ Range: _____

6) 0, 1, 14, 11, 8, 6, 8, 1, 5, 1

    Mode: _____ Range: _____

7) 4, 6, 2, 9, 7, 7, 6, 7, 3, 7

    Mode: _____ Range: _____

8) 9, 6, 4, 9, 6, 9, 9, 6, 3

    Mode: _____ Range: _____

9) 4, 4, 5, 8, 4, 4, 7, 8, 4, 10

    Mode: _____ Range: _____

10) 17, 9, 12, 9, 4, 9, 18, 10

    Mode: _____ Range: _____

11) 14, 1, 17, 2, 2, 12, 28, 2

    Mode: _____ Range: _____

12) 6, 18, 15, 10, 6, 6, 3, 12

    Mode: _____ Range: _____

✍ Solve.

13) A stationery sold 13 pencils, 38 red pens, 49 blue pens, 13 notebooks, 39 erasers, 44 rulers and 42 color pencils. What are the Mode and Range for the stationery sells?

    Mode: _____   Range: _____

14) In an English test, eight students score 12, 10, 18, 12, 19, 20, 16 and 11. What are their Mode and Range? _____

Graph Points on a Coordinate Plane

✎ Plot each point on the coordinate grid.

1) A (5, 8)   3) C (2, 6)   5) E (1, 7)

2) B (4, 5)   4) D (7, 6)   6) F (8, 1)

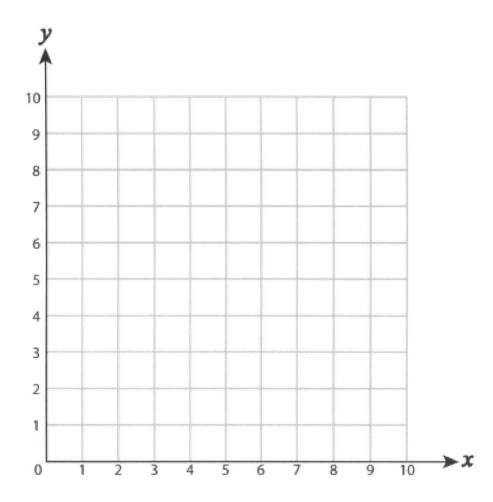

Bar Graph

✎ Graph the given information as a bar graph.

Day	Hot dogs sold
Monday	40
Tuesday	70
Wednesday	20
Thursday	90
Friday	60

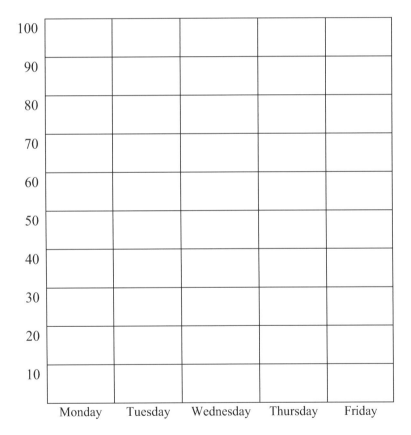

Tally and Pictographs

✎ Using the key, draw the pictograph to show the information.

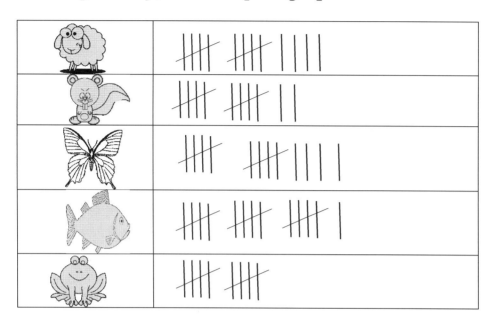

Key: ⚽ = 2 animals

Line Graphs

✍ David work as a salesman in a store. He records the number of shoes sold in five days on a line graph. Use the graph to answer the question

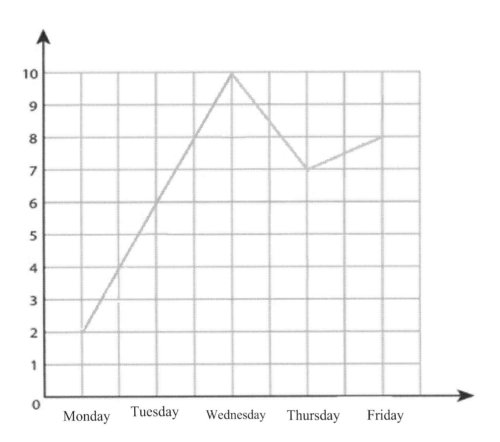

1) How many shoes were sold on Tuesday?

2) Which day had the minimum sales of shoes?

3) Which day had the maximum number of shoes sold?

4) How many shoes were sold in 5 days?

Stem–And–Leaf Plot

✎ Make stem ad leaf plots for the given data.

1) 32, 34, 37, 11, 12, 34, 58, 57, 39, 34, 18, 53

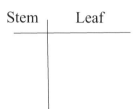

2) 21, 65, 32, 28, 25, 21, 31, 61, 69, 30, 65, 39

3) 122, 79, 96, 75, 100, 127, 92, 124, 78, 122, 98, 127

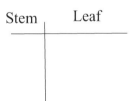

4) 64, 30, 100, 64, 72, 36, 109, 68, 75, 39, 68, 106, 70

Scatter Plots

✍ Construct a scatter plot.

x	1	2	3	4	5	8
y	20	30	45	60	80	10

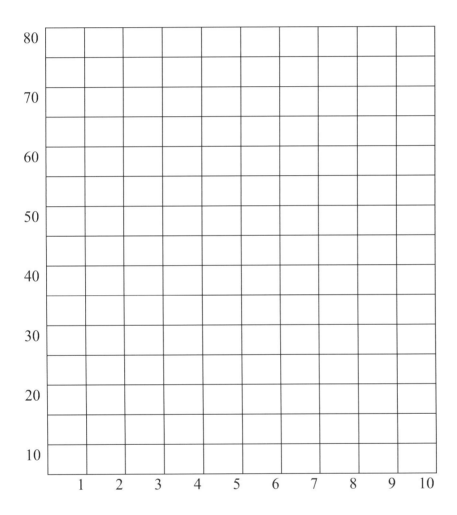

Probability Problems

✎Solve.

1) A number is chosen at random from 1 to 10. Find the probability of selecting a 5 or smaller.

2) A number is chosen at random from 1 to 45. Find the probability of selecting multiples of 15.

3) A number is chosen at random from 1 to 10. Find the probability of selecting multiples of 2 or 3.

4) A number is chosen at random from 1 to 10. Find the probability of selecting a multiple of 4.

5) A number is chosen at random from 1 to 20. Find the probability of selecting prime numbers.

6) A number is chosen at random from 1 to 15. Find the probability of not selecting factors of 12.

Answers of Worksheets – Chapter 12

Mean and Median

1) Mean: 10.2, Median: 9

2) Mean: 10, Median: 9

3) Mean: 13.2, Median: 13

4) Mean: 5, Median: 5.5

5) Mean: 8.1, Median: 8

6) Mean: 8.57, Median: 6

7) Mean: 11.75, Median: 8

8) Mean: 13, Median: 9

9) Mean: 38.14, Median: 38

10) Mean: 10, Median: 11

11) Mean: 39.5, Median: 38.5

12) Mean: 58, Median: 50.5

13) Mean:53.83, Median: 53.5

14) Mean: 70.14, Median: 82

15) Mean: 60.33, Median: 57

16) Mean: 39.14, Median: 20

Mode and Range

1) Mode: 3, Range: 7

2) Mode: 7, Range: 18

3) Mode: 2, Range: 18

4) Mode: 29, Range: 27

5) Mode: 6, Range: 14

6) Mode: 1, Range: 14

7) Mode: 7, Range: 7

8) Mode: 9, Range6

9) Mode: 4, Range: 6

10) Mode: 11, Range: 9.5

11) Mode: 2, Range: 27

12) Mode: 6, Range: 15

13) Mode: 13, Range: 36

14) Mode: 12, Range: 10

Graph Points on a Coordinate Plane

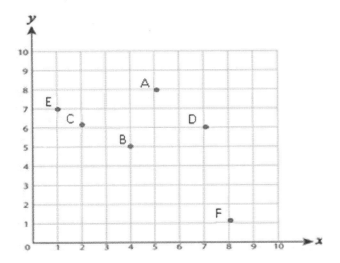

Bar Graph

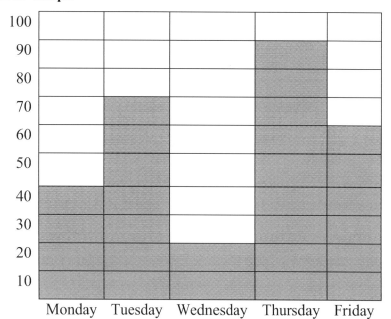

Tally and Pictographs

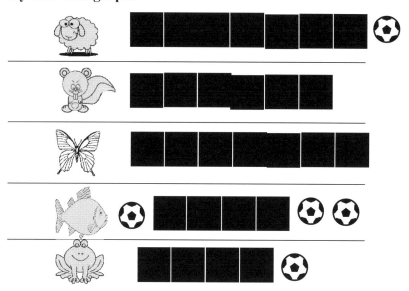

Line Graphs

1) 6   2) Monday   3) Wednesday   4) 33

Stem–And–Leaf Plot

1)

Stem	leaf
1	1 2 8
3	2 4 4 4 7 9
5	3 7 8

2)

Stem	leaf
2	1 1 5 8
3	0 1 2 9
6	1 5 5 9

3)

Stem	leaf
7	5 8 9
9	2 6 8
10	0
12	2 2 4 7 7

4)

Stem	leaf
3	0 6 9
6	4 4 8 8
7	0 2 5
10	0 6 9

Scatter Plots

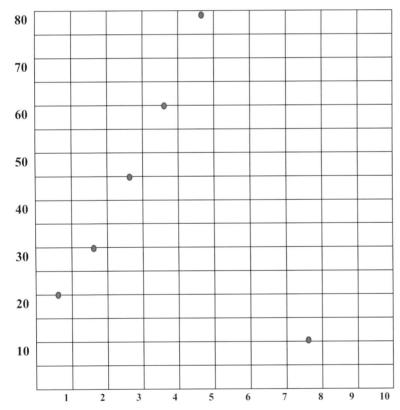

Probability Problems

1) $\frac{1}{2}$

2) $\frac{1}{15}$

3) $\frac{7}{10}$

4) $\frac{1}{5}$

5) $\frac{2}{5}$

6) $\frac{3}{5}$

SSAT Lower Level Practice Tests

The SSAT, or Secondary School Admissions Test, is a standardized test to help determine admission to private elementary, middle and high schools.

There are currently three Levels of the SSAT:

- ✓ Lower Level (for students in 3rd and 4th grade)
- ✓ Middle Level (for students in 5th-7th grade)
- ✓ Upper Level (for students in 8th-11th grade)

There are four sections on the SSAT Lower Level Test:

- ✓ Quantitative section: 30 questions, 30 minutes.
- ✓ Verbal section: 30 questions, 20 minutes.
- ✓ Reading section: 7 short passages, 28 questions, 30 minutes.
- ✓ Writing sample: 15 minutes to write a short passage

In this book, we have reviewed mathematics topics being tested on the quantitative (math) section of the SSAT Middle Level. In this section, there are two complete SSAT Lower Level Quantitative Tests. Let your student take these tests to see what score they will be able to receive on a real SSAT Lower Level test.

Time to Test

Time to refine your skill with a practice examination

Take a REAL SSAT Lower Level Mathematics test to simulate the test day experience. After you've finished, score your test using the answer key.

Before You Start

- You'll need a pencil and a timer to take the test.

- After you've finished the test, review the answer key to see where you went wrong.

- You will receive 1 point for every correct answer. You won't receive any point for wrong or skipped answers.

   Calculators are NOT permitted for the SSAT Lower Level Test

Good Luck!

SSAT Lower Level Practice Test Answer Sheets

Remove (or photocopy) these answer sheets and use them to complete the practice tests.

SSAT Lower Level Practice Test

Quantitative Section

1	Ⓐ Ⓑ Ⓒ Ⓓ Ⓔ	11	Ⓐ Ⓑ Ⓒ Ⓓ Ⓔ	21	Ⓐ Ⓑ Ⓒ Ⓓ Ⓔ
2	Ⓐ Ⓑ Ⓒ Ⓓ Ⓔ	12	Ⓐ Ⓑ Ⓒ Ⓓ Ⓔ	22	Ⓐ Ⓑ Ⓒ Ⓓ Ⓔ
3	Ⓐ Ⓑ Ⓒ Ⓓ Ⓔ	13	Ⓐ Ⓑ Ⓒ Ⓓ Ⓔ	23	Ⓐ Ⓑ Ⓒ Ⓓ Ⓔ
4	Ⓐ Ⓑ Ⓒ Ⓓ Ⓔ	14	Ⓐ Ⓑ Ⓒ Ⓓ Ⓔ	24	Ⓐ Ⓑ Ⓒ Ⓓ Ⓔ
5	Ⓐ Ⓑ Ⓒ Ⓓ Ⓔ	15	Ⓐ Ⓑ Ⓒ Ⓓ Ⓔ	25	Ⓐ Ⓑ Ⓒ Ⓓ Ⓔ
6	Ⓐ Ⓑ Ⓒ Ⓓ Ⓔ	16	Ⓐ Ⓑ Ⓒ Ⓓ Ⓔ	26	Ⓐ Ⓑ Ⓒ Ⓓ Ⓔ
7	Ⓐ Ⓑ Ⓒ Ⓓ Ⓔ	17	Ⓐ Ⓑ Ⓒ Ⓓ Ⓔ	27	Ⓐ Ⓑ Ⓒ Ⓓ Ⓔ
8	Ⓐ Ⓑ Ⓒ Ⓓ Ⓔ	18	Ⓐ Ⓑ Ⓒ Ⓓ Ⓔ	28	Ⓐ Ⓑ Ⓒ Ⓓ Ⓔ
9	Ⓐ Ⓑ Ⓒ Ⓓ Ⓔ	19	Ⓐ Ⓑ Ⓒ Ⓓ Ⓔ	29	Ⓐ Ⓑ Ⓒ Ⓓ Ⓔ
10	Ⓐ Ⓑ Ⓒ Ⓓ Ⓔ	20	Ⓐ Ⓑ Ⓒ Ⓓ Ⓔ	30	Ⓐ Ⓑ Ⓒ Ⓓ Ⓔ

SSAT Lower Level Practice Test 1

Quantitative Section

❖ **30 Questions.**

❖ **Total time for this test: 30 Minutes**.

❖ **You may NOT use a calculator for this test.**

Administered *Month Year*

1) Which of the following is closest to 8.04?

   A.8   A   D.8.4

B.8.2   E. 8.5

C.6

2) In the multiplication bellow, A represents which digit?

$$16 \times 5A4 = 8,544$$

A.4    B   D.7

B.3   E. 8

C.0

3) In the following figure, the shaded squares are what fractional part of the whole set of squares?

A.$\frac{1}{2}$ 4/12   D.$\frac{2}{3}$

B.$\frac{4}{8}$ C   E.$\frac{8}{12}$

C.$\frac{1}{3}$

4) Which of the following is greater than $\frac{12}{5}$?

A.$\frac{1}{2}$ D.2

B.$\frac{5}{2}$ B   E.2.3

C.$\frac{3}{4}$

5) If $8 \times (M + N) = 40$ and M is greater than 0, then N could Not be ….

A. 5

D. 3

B. 4

E. 1

C. 2

6) If $\frac{1}{4}$ of a number is greater than 7, the number must be ….

A. Less than 8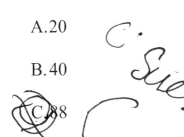

D. Greater than 28

B. Equal to 14

E. Equal to 30

C. Equal to 32

7) At a Zoo, the ratio of lions to tigers is 16 to 4. Which of the following could

NOT be the total number of lions and tigers in the zoo?

A. 20

D. 430

B. 40

E. 580

C. 88

8) Numbers x and y are shown below. How many times larger is the value of digit

8 in the number x, than the value of digit 8 in the number y?

$$x = 7,486 \quad y = 789$$

A. 10

D. 1,000

B. 1

E. 10,000

C. 100

9) If N is an even number, which of the following is always an odd number?

A. $\frac{2N}{4}$

C. $4N$

B. $N + 6$

D. $(2 \times N) + 2$

E. $N + 1$

 10) Which of the following expressions has the same value as $\frac{5}{2} \times \frac{8}{3}$?

A. $\frac{6 \times 5}{2}$

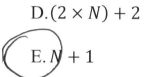

D. $\frac{5 \times 4}{3}$

B. $\frac{6 \times 2}{2}$

E. $\frac{8 \times 3}{2}$

C. $\frac{5 \times 6}{4}$

11) If 8 added to a number, the sum is 32. If the same number added to 12, the

answer is

A. 30

D. 36

B. 35

E. 45

C. 40

12) $\frac{2 + 5 + 7 \times 1 + 1}{4 + 8} = ?$

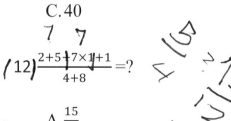

A. $\frac{15}{8}$

D. $\frac{8}{4}$

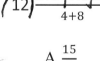 B. $\frac{4}{8}$

E. $\frac{5}{4}$

C. $\frac{5}{4}$

  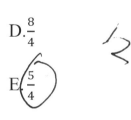

13) $8.5 - 3.08$ is closest to which of the following.

A. 4.1

D. 10

B. 5.4

E. 12

C. 5

14) What is the Area of the square shown in the following square?

5

A. 5

D. 18

B. 25

E. 12

C. 10

15) If 72 can be divided by both 9 and x without leaving a remainder, then 72 can also be divided by which of the following?

A. $x + 2$

D. $x \times 2$

B. $2x - 3$

E. $x + 5$

C. $x - 2$

16) Use the equations below to answer the question:

$$x + 16 = 19$$

$$15 + y = 20$$

What is the value of $x + y$?

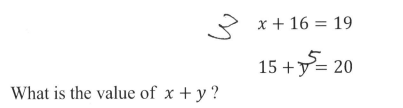

A. 9

D. 6

B. 10

E. 8

C. 8

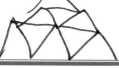

17) When 9 is added to four times number N, the result is 51. Then N is ….

    A. 12

    B. 6

    C. 8

    D. 12

    E. 14

18) At noon, the temperature was 30 degrees. By midnight, it had dropped another 35 degrees. What was the temperature at midnight?

    A. 5 degrees above zero

    B. 24 degrees below zero

    C. 10 degrees above zero

    D. 5 degrees below zero

    E. 10 degrees below zero

19) If a triangle has a base of 8 cm and a height of 11 cm, what is the area of the triangle?

    A. $44 cm^2$

    B. $25 cm^2$

    C. $24 cm^2$

    D. $45 cm^2$

    E. $50 cm^2$

20) What is the next number in this sequence?

$$3, 7, 12, 18, 25, \dots$$

    A. 33

    B. 27

    C. 25

    D. 22

    E. 21

21) Which formula would you use to find the area of a square?

A. $length \times width \times height$

B. $side \times side$

C. $length \times width$

D. $\frac{1}{2} base \times height$

E. $\frac{1}{2}(length \times width \times heigt)$

22) What is the average of the following numbers?

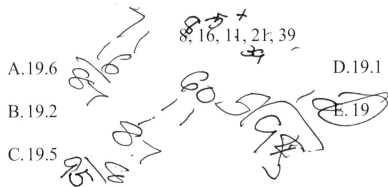

8, 16, 11, 21, 39

A. 19.6　　　　　　　　　　　　　　D. 19.1

B. 19.2　　　　　　　　　　　　　　E. 19

C. 19.5

23) Which of the following statement is False?

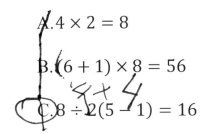

A. $4 \times 2 = 8$　　　　　　　　　D. $6 \times (5 - 2) = 18$

B. $(6 + 1) \times 8 = 56$　　　　　　E. $(10 + 19) \times 10 = 290$

C. $8 \div 2(5 - 1) = 16$

24) If all the sides in the following figure are of equal length and length of one

side is 8, what is the perimeter of the figure?

A. 15　　　　　　　　　　　　　　D. 48

B. 16　　　　　　　　　　　　　　E. 38

C. 20

25) If there are 7 red balls and 14 blue balls in a basket, what is the probability that John will pick out a red ball from the basket?

A. $\frac{16}{10}$

D. $\frac{3}{5}$

B. $\frac{2}{5}$

E. $\frac{20}{10}$

C. $\frac{1}{3}$

26) How many lines of symmetry does an equilateral triangle have?

A. 5

D. 2

B. 4

E. 1

C. 3

27) What is %30 of 300?

A. 10

D. 50

B. 60

E. 90

C. 20

28) Four people can paint 5 houses in 12 days. How many people are needed to paint 10 houses in 6 days?

A. 6

D. 4

B. 16

E. 20

C. 12

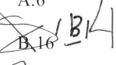    

29) $\frac{6}{8} - \frac{5}{8} = ?$

A. 0.125

D. 0.35

B. 0.215

E. 0.512

C. 0.25

30) If $N = 2$ and $\frac{32}{N} + 8 = \square$, then $\square = \dots$

A. 18

D. 30

B. 32

E. 24

C. 34

SSAT Lower Level Practice Test 2

Quantitative Section

- ❖ **30 Questions.**
- ❖ **Total time for this test: 30 Minutes**.
- ❖ **You may NOT use a calculator for this test.**

Administered *Month Year*

1) Find the missing number in the sequence: 5, 9, 14, ..., 27

A. 17

D. 16

B. 21

E. 18

C. 20

2) What is the value of x in the following math equation?

$$\frac{x}{12} + 24 = 30$$

A. 20

D. 48

B. 18

E. 45

C. 72

3) When 38 is divided by 6, the remainder is the same as when 44 is divided by

A. 5

D. 7

B. 6

E. 4

C. 2

4) The area of each square in the following shape is $9cm^2$. What is the area of shaded squares?

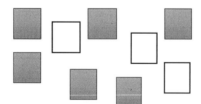

A. 45 cm^2

D. 36cm^2

B. 63cm^2

E. 54cm^2

C. 48cm^2

5) $\frac{10}{3} - \frac{4}{3} = ?$

A. 1   D. 2.5

B. 1.5   E. 3

C. 2

6) If $64 = 6 \times N + 16$, then $N = \dots$

A. 8   D. 15

B. 12   E. 20

C. 14

7) When 8 is added to six times a number N, the result is 20. Which of the following equations represents this statement?

A. $6 + 8N = 20$ D. $6N + 20 = 8$

B. $20N + 6 = 8$ E. $8N + 20 = 6$

C. $6N + 8 = 20$

8) John has 2,400 cards and Max has 604 cards. How many more cards does John have than Max?

A. 1,796   D. 1,688

B. 1,696   E. 1,969

C. 1,766

9) What is 4 percent of 550?

A. 20

D. 22

B. 24

E. 32

C. 25

10) In a basket, the ratio of red marbles to blue marbles is 5 to 2. Which of the following could NOT be the total number of red and blue marbles in the basket?

A. 28

D. 14

B. 77

E. 34

C. 42

11) A square has an area of $36cm^2$. What is its perimeter?

A. 28 cm^2

D. 40 cm^2

B. 24 cm^2

E. 36 cm^2

C. 32 cm^2

12) The length of a rectangle is 6 times of its width. If the length is 12, what is the perimeter of the rectangle?

A. 30

D. 28

B. 62

E. 32

C. 24

13) In the following right triangle, what is the value of x?

A. 15

B. 30

C. 45

D. 60

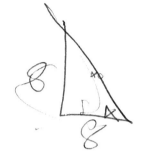
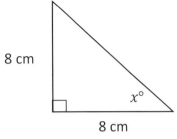

8 cm

8 cm

$x°$

E. It cannot be determined from the information given

14) Mary has y dollars. John has $16 more than Mary. If John gives Mary $25, then in terms of y, how much does John have now?

A. $y + 4$

B. $y + 5$

C. $y - 5$

D. $y - 9$

E. $y + 8$

15) Dividing 107 by 6 leaves a remainder of

A. 4

B. 2

C. 3

D. 5

E. 2

16) If $7,000 + A - 300 = 8,100$, then $A =$

A. 600

B. 500

C. 1,500

D. 2,100

E. 3,000

17) For what price is 35 percent off the same as $84 off?

    A. $150   84   D. $200   yes sir

    B. $300   E. $240

    C. $260

18) Which of the following fractions is less than $\frac{7}{4}$?

    A. 1.4 $1\frac{3}{4}$ C. 3

    B. $\frac{7}{2}$ a   D. 2.8

                       E. 4.2   I Don't need a mo

              230

19) If $420 - x + 116 = 240$, then $x =$

    A. 205   230   440   D. 215

    B. 168   116   114   E. 316

C   C. 306   114 30

20) Of the following, 50 percent of $87.99 is closest to

    A. $12.90   43.   D. $25.50

    B. $22.00 $2\overline{)87.99}$ E. $16.00

    C. $44.00

21) Solve.

                  $8.08 - 4.6 = \dots$

                7

    A. 3.24   8.08   D. 3

    B. 3.42   4.6   E. 3.4

    C. 3.48   3.48

22) If $900 + \square - 380 = 1,400$, then $\square = ?$

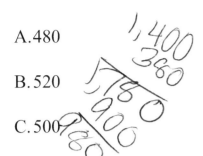

    A. 480   D. 880

    B. 520   E. 645

    C. 500

23) There are 85 students in a class. If the ratio of the number of girls to the total number of students in the class is $\frac{1}{5}$, which are the following is the number of boys in that class?

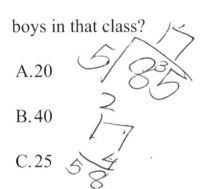 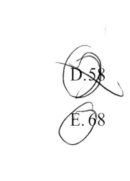

    A. 20   D. 58

    B. 40   E. 68

    C. 25

24) If $N \times (9 - 7) = 16$ then $N = ?$

    A. 8   D. 18

    B. 16   E. 13

    C. 12

25) If $x \blacksquare y = 4x + y - 4$, what is the value of $2 \blacksquare 12$?

    A. 3   D. 25

    B. 15   E. 46

    C. 16

26) Which of the following statements is False?

A. $(5 \times 2 + 12) \times 2 = 44$ D. $4 \times (4 + 4) = 32$

B. $(4 \times 5 + 8) \div 2 = 14$ E. $14 \div (5 + 2) = 3$

C. $7 + (3 \times 2) = 12$

27) Of the following, which number if the greatest?

A. 0.082   D. 0.8986

B. 0.8922   E. 0.88

C. 0.8913

28) $\frac{7}{8} - \frac{3}{4} =$

A. 0.125   D. 0.426

B. 0.135   E. 0.146

C. 0.5

29) Which of the following is the closest to 8.03?

A. 8   D. 8.5

B. 8.2   E. 6.5

C. 8.3

30) Use the equation below to answer the question.

$$x + 15 = 7$$
$$9y = 27$$

What is the value of $y - x$?

A. 1   D. 4

B. 2   E. 7

C. 5

Score Your Test

ores are broken down by its three sections: Verbal, Quantitative (or Math),

ling. A sum of the three sections is also reported.

$SAT lower level, the score range is 300-600, the lowest possible score a

can earn is 300 and the highest score is 600 for each section. A student

es 1 point for every correct answer. For SSAT Lower Level, there is no

y for wrong answers. That means that you can calculate the raw score by

together the number of right answers.

tal scaled score for a Lower Level SSAT is the sum of the scores for the

ative, verbal, and reading sections. A student will also receive a percentile

between 1-99% that compares that student's test scores with those of other

rs of same grade and gender from the past 3 years.

llowing table to convert SSAT Lower Level Quantitative Reasoning raw

aled score.

2 no 3

SSAT Lowe Level Quantitative Reasoning raw score to scaled score	
Raw Scores	Scaled Scores
Below 10	Below 400
11 − 15	410 − 450
16 − 20	560 − 500
21 − 25	510 − 550
26 − 30	560 − 600

9

10